CW00321723

CHARMING
SMALL HOTEL
GUIDES

Tuscany &
Umbria

including Florence and Siena

CHARMING SMALL HOTEL GUIDES

Tuscany & Umbria

including Florence and Siena

DUNCAN PETERSEN

Conceived, designed and produced by
Duncan Petersen Publishing Ltd

Author	Peter Kennealy
Revisions Editors	Jon Eldon
	Nicola Davies
Guest contributors	Nicola Swallow, Richard Dixon,
	Fiona Duncan
Editorial Director	Andrew Duncan
Art Director	Mel Petersen

This edition published in the UK and Commonwealth 1999 by
Duncan Petersen Publishing Ltd,
31 Ceylon Road, London W14 OPY.

This is a reprint with corrections of the first edition of this guide,
written by Peter Kennealy, Richard Dixon, Nicola Swallow and
Fiona Duncan in 1995. Peter Kennealy and the other writers were
not involved in the revisions made for this reprint and take no
responsibility for errors, ommissions or judgements expressed.

Sales representation and distribution in the UK and Ireland by
Portfolio Books Limited
Unit 1C, West Ealing Business Centre
Alexandria Road
London W13 0NJ
Tel: 0181 579 7748

ISBN 1 872576 81 8

A CIP catalogue record for this book is available
from the British Library

Published in the USA by
Hunter Publishing Inc.,
130 Campus Drive, Edison, N.J. 08818.
Tel (732) 225 1900 Fax (732) 417 0482

For details on hundreds of other travel guides and language
courses, visit Hunter's Web site at
http://www.hunterpublishing.com

ISBN 1-55650-870-9

Printed by Estudios gráficos Zure S.A., Spain

Contents

Introduction

Welcome to this updated reprint of the first regional guide in the now well-established *Charming Small Hotel Guides series*. In covering an area, rather than a whole country, we did so in depth, using only a few of the places featured in our all-Italy guide - those entries we could not ignore. The majority of the places featured in this guide do not appear in our all-Italy guide.

Peter Kennealy, the original author of this guide, was unable to work on this revision.

Charming and small
There really are relatively few *genuine charming* small hotels. Unlike other guides, we are particularly fussy about size. In Italy, even family-run hotels seem to grow inevitably and the ten-room hotel is a rarity, but most of our recommendations have fewer than 30 rooms. If a hotel has more than that, it needs to have the feel of a much smaller place to be in this guide.

We attach more importance to size than other guides because we think that unless a hotel is small, it cannot give a genuinely personal welcome, or make you feel like an individual, rather than just a guest. For what we mean by a personal welcome, see below.

Unlike other gudes, we often rule out places that have great qualitites, but are nonetheless no more nor less than – hotels. Our hotels are all special in some way.

We think that we have a much clearer idea than other guides of what is special and what is not; and we think we apply these criteria more consistently than other guides because we are a small and personally managed company rather than a bureaucracy. We have a small team of like-minded inspectors, chosen by the editor and thoroughly rehearsed in recognizing what we want. While we very much appreciate reader' reports – see page 182 – they are not our main source of information.

Last but by no means least, we're independent – there's no payment for inclusion.

So what exactly do we look for?
• An attractive, preferably peaceful setting.
• A building that is either handsome or interesting or historic, or at least with a distinct character.
• Ideally, we look for adequate space, but on a human scale: we don't go for places that rely on grandeur, or that have pretensions that could intimidate.
• Decoration must be harmonious and in good taste, and the furnishings and facilities comfortable and well maintained. We like to see interesting antique furniture that is there because it can be used, not simply revered.
• The proprietors and staff need to be dedicated and

Introduction

thoughtful, offering a personal welcome, without being intrusive. The guest needs to feel like an individual.

Tuscany and Umbria for the traveller

It is not difficult to recognize why we chose Tuscany and Umbria as the first regional guide for the series. The region is favoured, *par excellence,* both with natural and man-made landscapes of incomparable beauty and variety, and its artistic heritage is unequalled in the world. From the Tuscan Coast with its white beaches and pine-shaded coasts to Chianti's rolling hills teeming with cypresses, olives and vines to Umbria, Italy's green heart, visitors will find any form of nature to suit their taste. Travellers through the Garfagnana, in the north-western corner of Tuscany, often think that they have accidentally strayed into some dramatic part of the Alps; while in the still under-explored Maremma, to the south-west, they find cowboys on horse-back tending their herds.

Dotted across the whole region are, of course, many of Italy's most famous *citta d'arte* (art cities), whose names everone knows: Florence, Siena, Volterra, San Gimignano, Perugia, Assisi and Gubbio. But these are only the diamonds in the tiara (and perhaps suffering in recent years from the depredations of mass tourism – they are best seen out of high season unless your idea of a holiday is to stand in long queues for a three-minute ogle of David).

Less well-known gems abound throughout the two regions: Montefalco, known as Umbria's balcony for its remarkable outlook; Trevi, with its dramatic mountain-side location; Pienza, a delightful and unique remainder of Renaissance town planning; and San Piero a Sieve, in the Mugello, whose ugly outskirts belie its medieval heart.

Much of the delight of travelling this region lies in ignoring the standard tourist trails and just following the road. Do this, and you will always be sure of arriving at some memorable destination which, may well not yet be 'discovered' – by the tourists, or the guide books.

Entries, long and short

The full-page entries with colour photographs are our warmest recommendations **BUT** the short (three-a-page) entries on pages 145-181 are all charming small hotels, and by no means second class. Think of them as silver- or bronze-medallists (a world full of gold medallists would be intolerably boring). They have all, like the long entries, been inspected, and selected for inclusion in the guide because they satisfy our criteria.

Hotels, villas, *locande, agriturismo,*

The range of accommodation on offer in Tuscany and

Introduction

Umbria should be enough to satisfy all tastes and most pockets, with a variety of names almost as numerous as those describing types of pasta. 'Hotel' is common enough, but so is its Italian equivalent *'albergo'*. 'Villa' can apply either to a town or country hotel and is used by proprietors with some latitude: occasionally one wonders why a nondescript town house or farmhouse should be called a villa while a more elegant building restricts itself to *albergo*. *'Palazzo'* and *'pensione'* generally refer to urban accommodation while *'agriturismo'* means farmhouse bed-and-breakfast, or indeed, self-catering apartments. *'Residence'*, *'relais'*, *'locanda'*, *'castello'* and *'fattoria'* are also found.

The variety that one finds under these various names is extraordinary, from world-ranking luxury hotels to relatively simple guest-houses.

Bedrooms and bathrooms
Most of the hotels in this guide are found in old buildings, whether they be farmhouses, medieval castles or towers, Renaissance villas and *palazzi*, former monasteries or just a solid edifice from the 19thC. This guarantees individuality, but it also means that, in the same hotel, the standards of rooms can vary greatly, as, occasionally, do prices. When writing to the hotel, state your requirements - not every monk's cell in a former monastery is blessed with a view. And neither, originally, would it have had a bath room *en suite*. For the most part, these have been added without undue intrusiveness, but they tend not to be spacious, at least by American standards.

Style varies, but Italians are a meticulously clean people and no bedrooms and bathrooms should be less than acceptable.

Meals
Strangely enough, the one place in Italy where a cup of coffee can be disappointing is in a hotel. The pre-prepared beverage lacks the intense flavour of a freshly-made *espresso* or steaming *cappuccino*, so if you are fussy about your first cup of the day, ask for one of these. Bed-and-breakfasts tend to serve 'moka' coffee, made in the characteristic aluminium pot found in all Italian households. In hotels, self-service buffet breakfasts are common, with everything available from cereals to salami, and are ideal for travellers who

---

No fear, no favour
This is an independent guide. The selection is based on personal recommendation and expert assessment by the editors and a small team of helpers.
No establishment pays to be in this guide.

---

may not eat properly again until the evening. Most Italians start the day with a *cappuccino* and a brioche, and in some establishments this may be all you are offered.

Half board is rarely obligatory and often not available, even if the hotel has a restaurant attached, as most visitors like to sample the wide variety of restaurants in an area.

Your host and hostess

Nearly every place we visited claimed to speak English, though sometimes it was not clear what level of fluency was involved. Do not worry: the more professional hotels all have staff with some degree of proficiency and for the rest, Italians are irrepressible communicators across any number of linguistic and cultural barriers. If you can offer a few phrases of Italian, it will usually work wonders.

Travel facts

The tourist information offices for each province are listed with the relevant maps on pages 14-32. Most cities and a few popular towns also have their own tourist offices offering information on local travel, museums, galleries and fiestas.

Flights

The principal airports for Tuscany are at Pisa and Florence, and car hire is available at both. Pisa airport is connected directly to Florence by an hourly train service. Florence airport has a less satisfactory bus connection to the centre. If you are staying in town, try to share a taxi.
Umbria has no major airport of its own, but there is a small one near Perugia. You can fly there from Pisa or Florence airports, or from Rome or Rimini.

Pets

Even if the fact box following the description says 'pets accepted', please notify when booking that you want to take a pet. No hotelier wants a pack of hounds racing around the foyer, and many only allow small dogs, kept exclusively to the guest's own room.

Electricity

The norm is 220-volt-50-cycles. U.S. visitors will need electrical converters (or dual voltage appliances). Most bathrooms do not supply hair-driers. Two plug sizes operate in Italy, so be sure to bring an adaptor.

Introduction

Smoking
Nobody seems to know what the law is, or how it should be interpreted, and at the time of writing a free-for-all reigns with very few exceptions. Some hotels have a non-smoking area; it may be the case that by the time this guide is published smoking will be banned in public places, although it would be naive to expect this rule to be rigorously observed.

How to find an entry
In the first part of the guide are the long entries, first in Tuscany, then in Umbria.

Within these sections, the hotels are listed alphabetically, **1** by province; **2** by town or local government district (*comune*); and **3** by the name of the hotel. The short entries at the back of the guide are organized in a similar way.
There are three easy ways to find a hotel:

* Use the maps on pages 14-32. Each number on a map refers to the page on which the hotel is featured.

* If you know the area you want to visit, browse through that section until you find a place that meets your requirements.

* Use the indexes at the back of the book. They list entries both by hotel name (pages 183-186) and by location (pages 187-190).

How to read an entry
At the top of each page is the relevant region (Tuscany or Umbria); below that is the province; then follows the type of hotel and its town or district and, finally, the name of the hotel itself.

In the case of Florence, which is both the largest city and an important province, we use the English name for the town and the Italian name, Firenze, for the province.
The description then follows.

Fact boxes
Following the description are facts and figures that should help you to decide if the hotel is in your price range and has the facilities you want.

First comes the the **address**. 'Loc.' stands for locality (*localitá* in Italian) and indicates the area near a town where the hotel is situated. The name of the town is generally the name of the *comune* (the local administrative unit) and these can cover quite a large area, especially in rural parts. You should be armed with a map. We recommend the *Atlante Stradale d'Italia - Centro*, published by the Touring Club Italiano.

Introduction

The address concludes with the postal code and the name of the province (abbreviated in Italian to a two-letter code).

Tel and fax
The number in brackets is the area code within Italy. If you are calling from abroad, you must include the zero after the international code for Italy (39).

Location
The location and setting of the hotel are briefly described; car parking facilities follow. In Florence, few hotels have their own car parking, and depend on arrangements with nearby garages. The prices are set by the garages and not by the hotels, so please check first.

Prices
The range of prices is from the cheapest single room in low season to the most expensive double in high season.

up to 150,000 lire	L
150 - 250,000 lire	LL
250 - 350,000 lire	LLL
over 350,000 lire	LLLL

Prices have been calculated to include VAT and breakfast. (In some cases, the hotels already include breakfast in their standard rates; in others, they charge a hefty supplement. For reasons of comparability, we have taken this into account when placing the hotel within our price bands.)

In cases where hotels have suites available at a higher price, we have indicated this with an additional price band (e.g. L-LL -LLL). Prices for half board are per person and are indicated with the symbols (DB&B).

Prices for **apartments** are also calculated on the basis of cost per person, per day. Undoubtedly, these represent excellent value (especially for families) and normally fall within our lower price band. However, please remember that a full range of hotel services will not be available and that there are minimum-stay requirements, usually three days in low season and a week during the busy period. Full details of booking deposits can be obtained from the owners.

Caution Hotels, especially in Florence, sometimes charge more than their advertised rates in high season, when there is competition for rooms. Occasionally, you may find that the price asked is higher than that indicated by our price bands.

Introduction

Rooms

Italian hotels can be exasperatingly vague on the number of rooms they have, especially in the more modest family-run establishments.

This may be a tax dodge (farmhouse bed-and-breakfasts are not supposed to have more than a certain number in order to benefit from financial concessions); it may also be a question of flexibility: a suite may be rented out as a standard double, or a three-day minimum stay waived in low season. It may be worth telephoning or faxing to ask for further details of rooms.

Facilities

We list public rooms plus outdoor and sporting facilities belonging to the hotel as well as any in the vicinity.

Credit cards

We use the following abbreviations for credit cards:
AE American Express
DC Diners Club
EC Eurocard
MC Master Card
V   Visa/Barclaycard/Bank Americard/Carte Bleue/Carta Si

Credit cards are now more widely accepted in Italy than before, with the exception of farmhouse bed-and-breakfasts, which prefer cash or travellers' cheques. The least accepted credit card is Diners Club.

Children

Children are nearly always welcome in Italian hotels (and restaurants). Some hotels clearly wish to offer their guests plenty of peace and quiet, and therefore discourage too many mini-guests. Others generally offer discounts on third beds in the room.

Disabled

'No special facilities' is too frequent a comment under this heading, but understandable if you consider the buildings in which the hotels are located. Many of our entries are planning installation of special bathrooms and ramps for ease of access, but centuries-old buildings can prove intractable in these matters.

Closed

March to November is the important season for Tuscan and Umbrian hotels and many close for the winter months (except for a couple of weeks around Christmas and the New Year). In and near the main cities, hotels are open the whole year around to cater for domestic tourism and numerous congresses.

Introduction

We list below Italy's official public holidays when banks and shops are shut and levels of public transport reduced. In Tuscany and Umbria, like the rest of the country, most towns have their own local holidays, usually the feast day of the patron saint, often celebrated with a fair and fireworks.

In addition to these are traditional events and festivals peculiar to each locality: Siena has its famous horse-race in Piazza del Campo (the Palio); in Arezzo, they joust in full medieval costumes; in Florence, they still play a lethal version of traditional football (*calcio in costume*); in Gubbio, teams of young men run up and down a steep mountain carrying gigantic wooden 'candles', apparently just for the fun of it. Religious pageantry is particularly rich around Easter and food and wine get their turn in the autumn with fairs ('sagre') devoted to tasting of local specialities: Chianti Classico, truffles (in Umbria), pecorino cheese (in the Pienza area), boar, and olive oil. Details can be had from local tourist offices, or keep an eye out for posters.

New Year's Day (*Capodanno*) Jan 1; Epiphany (*Epifania*) Jan 6; Holy Friday (*Venerdí Santo*); Easter Sunday (*Pasqua*); Easter Monday (*Pasquetta*); Liberation Day (*Liberazione*) April 25; May Day (*Festa del Lavoro*) May 1; Assumption of the Virgin (*Ferragosto*) Aug 15; All Saints' Day (*Tutti Santi*) Nov 1; Immaculate Conception (*Immacolata Concezione*) Dec 8; Christmas Day (*Natale*) Dec 25; St. Stephen's Day (*Santo Stefano*) Dec 26.

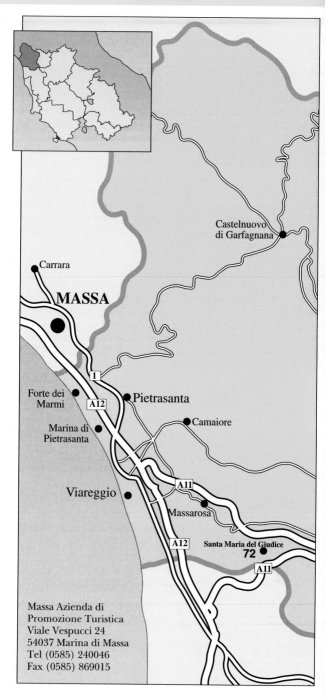

Castelnuovo
di Garfagnana

Carrara

MASSA

Forte dei
Marmi

Pietrasanta

Camaiore

Marina di
Pietrasanta

Viareggio

Massarosa

Santa Maria del Giudice
72

Massa Azienda di
Promozione Turistica
Viale Vespucci 24
54037 Marina di Massa
Tel (0585) 240046
Fax (0585) 869015

Lucca

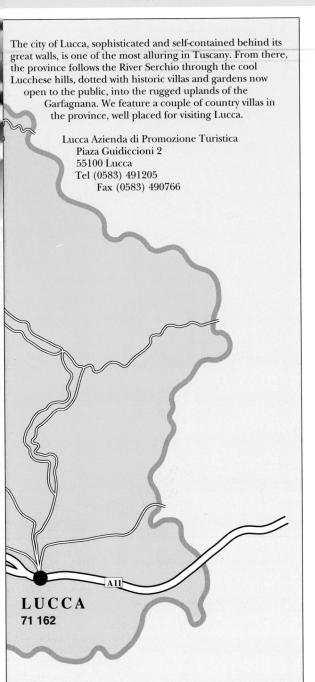

The city of Lucca, sophisticated and self-contained behind its great walls, is one of the most alluring in Tuscany. From there, the province follows the River Serchio through the cool Lucchese hills, dotted with historic villas and gardens now open to the public, into the rugged uplands of the Garfagnana. We feature a couple of country villas in the province, well placed for visiting Lucca.

Lucca Azienda di Promozione Turistica
Piaza Guidiccioni 2
55100 Lucca
Tel (0583) 491205
Fax (0583) 490766

A11

LUCCA
71 162

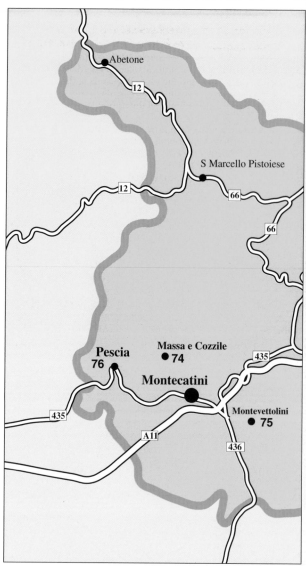

The little city of Pistoia, with its quintessential medieval square, its wealth of charming churches (containing three important early Renaissance pulpits) and its enchanting della Robbia frieze across the Ospedale del Ceppo, is one of the best-kept secrets in Tuscany. It has the added advantage of being a well-placed base for visiting Pisa, Lucca and Florence. The surrounding Pistoian hills are serenely peaceful, and we have several agreeable places to stay at in these hills, including self-catering apartments, bed-and-breakfasts and hotels proper, including one real gem.

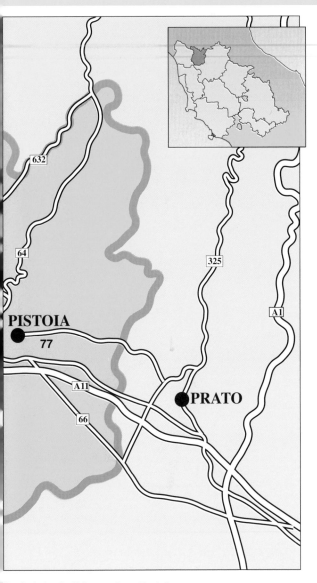

Pistoia Azienda di Promozione Turistica
Via Marconi 28
San Marcello Pistoiese
51028 Pistoia
Tel (0573) 630145
Fax (0573) 622120

Prato

Though the cities of Prato and Florence lie within a few miles of one another, they are like chalk and cheese. The Pratese roll their sleeves up and get their hands dirty (mostly in the textile industry on which Prato has grown rich), whilst the Florentines prefer to pursue a more aesthetic line of endeavour. 'Lazy', say the Pratese of the Florentines; 'philistines', say the Florentines of the Pratese. Casual tourists wouldn't know about Prato, whizzing past as they do on their way to Florence. Industrial though it is, it has a pleasant, down-to-earth air and some outstanding sights, including the exterior pulpit on the Duomo, where the sacred Virgin's Girdle is displayed five times a year. To the south of Prato there are notable villas at Poggio a Caiano and at Artimino; to the north, pleasant, hilly country merges into the Appenine foothills.

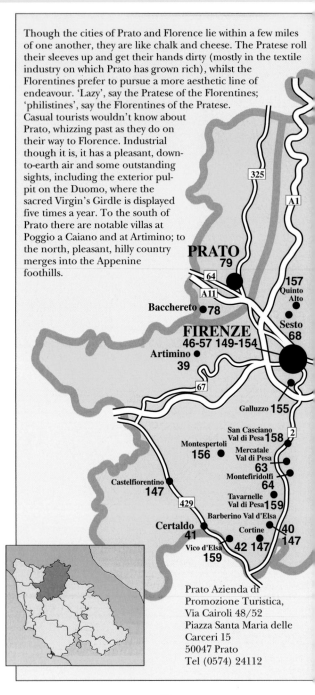

325

A1

PRATO
79

64

A11

157
Quinto
Alto

Bacchereto ● 78

FIRENZE
46-57 149-154

Sesto
68

Artimino ●
39

67

Galluzzo 155

2

San Casciano
Val di Pesa 158

Montespertoli
156 ●

Mercatale
Val di Pesa
63

Montefiridolfi
64

Castelfiorentino
147

Tavarnelle
Val di Pesa 159

429

Barberino Val d'Elsa

Certaldo
41

Cortine
42 147

40
147

Vico d'Elsa
159

Prato Azienda di
Promozione Turistica,
Via Cairoli 48/52
Piazza Santa Maria delle
Carceri 15
50047 Prato
Tel (0574) 24112

Firenze

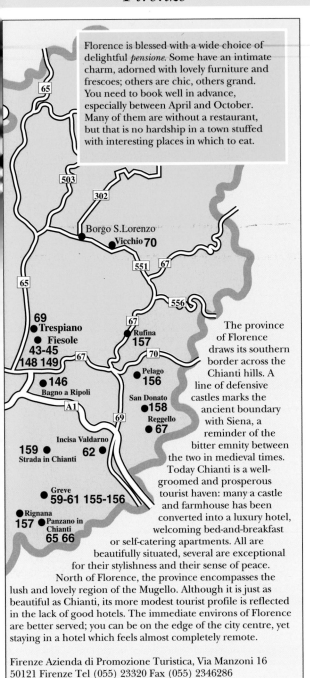

Florence is blessed with a wide choice of delightful *pensione*. Some have an intimate charm, adorned with lovely furniture and frescoes; others are chic, others grand. You need to book well in advance, especially between April and October. Many of them are without a restaurant, but that is no hardship in a town stuffed with interesting places in which to eat.

65

503

302

Borgo S.Lorenzo
● Vicchio **70**

551 67

556

65

69
● Trespiano
● **Fiesole**
43-45
148 149

67

67
● Rufina
157

70

● Pelago
156

● **146**
Bagno a Ripoli

A1

San Donato
● **158**

69

Reggello
● **67**

159
Strada in Chianti

Incisa Valdarno
62 ●

Greve
● **59-61 155-156**

● Rignana
157 ● Panzano in
Chianti
65 66

The province of Florence draws its southern border across the Chianti hills. A line of defensive castles marks the ancient boundary with Siena, a reminder of the bitter emnity between the two in medieval times. Today Chianti is a well-groomed and prosperous tourist haven: many a castle and farmhouse has been converted into a luxury hotel, welcoming bed-and-breakfast or self-catering apartments. All are beautifully situated, several are exceptional for their stylishness and their sense of peace.

North of Florence, the province encompasses the lush and lovely region of the Mugello. Although it is just as beautiful as Chianti, its more modest tourist profile is reflected in the lack of good hotels. The immediate environs of Florence are better served; you can be on the edge of the city centre, yet staying in a hotel which feels almost completely remote.

Firenze Azienda di Promozione Turistica, Via Manzoni 16
50121 Firenze Tel (055) 23320 Fax (055) 2346286

Arezzo

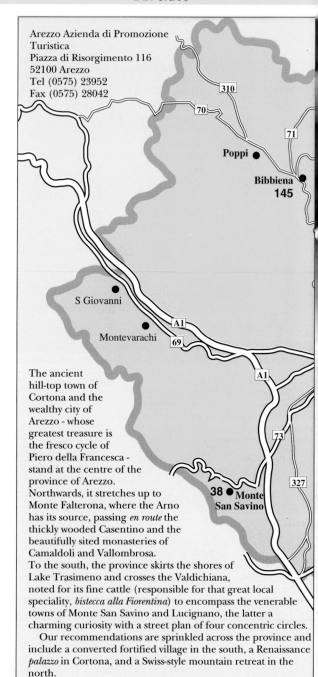

Arezzo Azienda di Promozione
Turistica
Piazza di Risorgimento 116
52100 Arezzo
Tel (0575) 23952
Fax (0575) 28042

310

70

71

Poppi ●

Bibbiena
145 ●

● S Giovanni

● Montevarachi

A1

69

A1

73

327

The ancient
hill-top town of
Cortona and the
wealthy city of
Arezzo - whose
greatest treasure is
the fresco cycle of
Piero della Francesca -
stand at the centre of the
province of Arezzo.
Northwards, it stretches up to
Monte Falterona, where the Arno
has its source, passing *en route* the
thickly wooded Casentino and the
beautifully sited monasteries of
Camaldoli and Vallombrosa.

38 ● **Monte
San Savino**

To the south, the province skirts the shores of
Lake Trasimeno and crosses the Valdichiana,
noted for its fine cattle (responsible for that great local
speciality, *bistecca alla Fiorentina*) to encompass the venerable
towns of Monte San Savino and Lucignano, the latter a
charming curiosity with a street plan of four concentric circles.

Our recommendations are sprinkled across the province and
include a converted fortified village in the south, a Renaissance
palazzo in Cortona, and a Swiss-style mountain retreat in the
north.

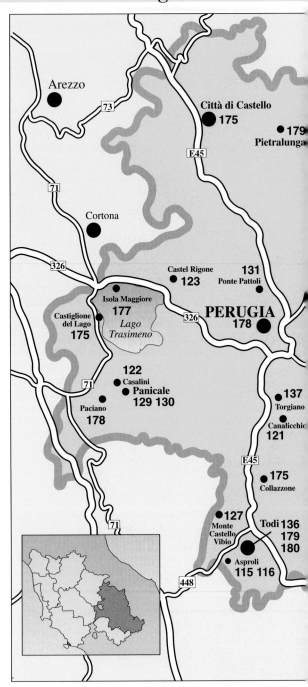

Arezzo

73

Città di Castello
175

179
Pietralunga

E45

71

Cortona

326

Castel Rigone
123

131
Ponte Pattoli

Isola Maggiore
177

326

PERUGIA
178

Castiglione
del Lago
175

*Lago
Trasimeno*

122
Casalini
71
Panicale
129 130

Paciano
178

137
Torgiano

Canalicchio
121

E45

175
Collazzone

71

127
Monte
Castello
Vibio

Todi 136
179
180

Asproli
115 116

448

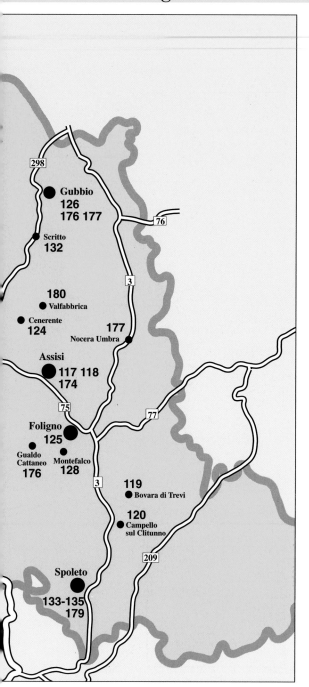

298

Gubbio
126
176 177

76

Scritto
132

3

180
● Valfabbrica

● Cenerente
124

177
Nocera Umbra ●

Assisi
117 118
174

75

77

Foligno
125

Gualdo
Cattaneo   Montefalco
176   **128**

3

119
● Bovara di Trevi

120
● Campello
sul Clitunno

209

Spoleto

133-135
179

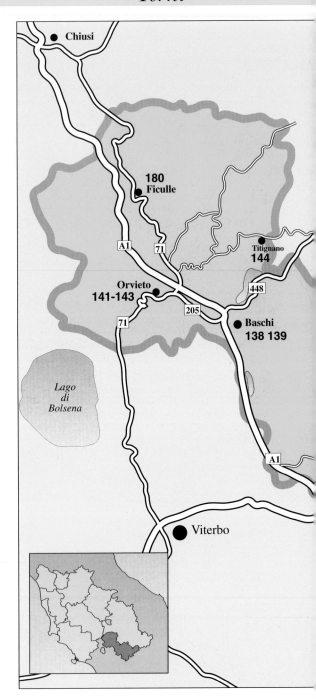

Chiusi

180
Ficulle

A1   71

Titignano
144

Orvieto
141-143

448

205

71

● **Baschi**
138 139

*Lago
di
Bolsena*

A1

● Viterbo

Terni

Though the city of Terni itself is an industrial blackspot, the small southern Umbrian province which takes its name includes some unsung towns such as Narni, Amelia and Baschi. It also includes Orvieto, secure on its volcanic crag and dominated by its great Gothic cathedral. As well as establishments in quiet rural backwaters, we have superbly situated hotels in Orvieto, as well as Narni and Baschi, which is close to the little Lago di Corbara, with its shores of red rock.

Terni Azienda di Promozione Turistica
Piazza Duomo 24
Orvieto 05018 Terni
Tel (0763) 42562
Fax (0763) 44433

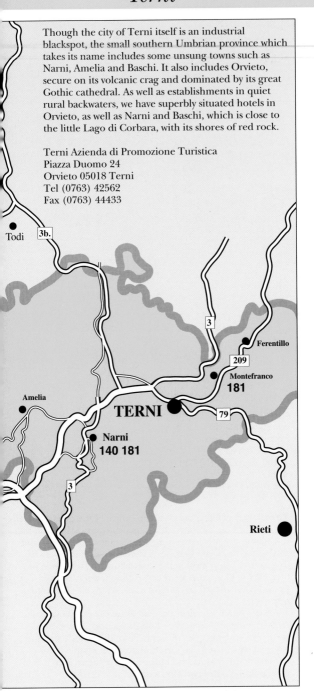

Todi

3b.

3

Ferentillo

209

Montefranco
181

Amelia

TERNI

79

Narni
140 181

3

Rieti

Siena

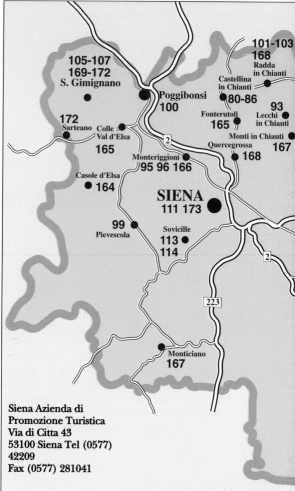

105-107
169-172
S. Gimignano

101-103
168
Radda
in Chianti

Castellina
in Chianti

Poggibonsi
100

80-86

93
Lecchi
in Chianti

Fonterutoli
165

172
Sarteano

Colle
Val d'Elsa
165

Monti in Chianti
Quercegrossa
168   167

Monteriggioni
95 96 166

Casole d'Elsa
164

SIENA
111 173

99
Pievescola

Sovicille
113
114

223

Monticiano
167

2

2

Siena Azienda di
Promozione Turistica
Via di Citta 43
53100 Siena Tel (0577)
42209
Fax (0577) 281041

The fair city of Siena stands at the centre of this geographically
varied province. To the east of Siena, the gentle vine-clad hills
of Chianti give way to the empty landscape of the Crete, and
further south, to the Val d'Orcia and the wooded slopes of
Tuscany's highest mountain, Monte Amiata. To the east of
Siena is San Gimignano, whose bristling towers and perfectly
preserved medieval streets have made it into a hollow tourist
trap.

Amongst our selection are the best of the farmhouses and
castles converted into stylish hotels which are now strewn
across the Chianti hills (others fall into the Firenze province,
pages 18-19) as well as a variety of accommodation in all
corners of the region, and in the towns of Siena, San
Gimignano, Pienza and Monteriggioni.

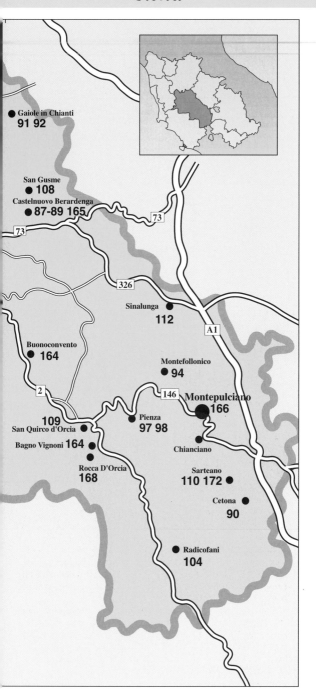

Gaiole in Chianti
91 92

San Gusme
● **108**
Castelnuovo Berardenga
● **87-89 165**

73

73

326

Sinalunga ●
112

A1

Buonoconvento
● **164**

Montefollonico
● **94**

146 Montepulciano
●**166**

Pienza
97 98

109
San Quirco d'Orcia ●
Bagno Vignoni **164** ●
Rocca D'Orcia
168

Chianciano ●

Sarteano
110 172 ●

Cetona ●
90

● Radicofani
104

2

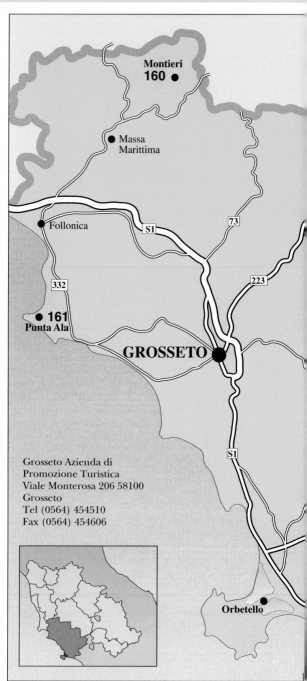

Montieri
160 ●

● Massa
Marittima

● Follonica   S1

73

332

● **161**
Punta Ala

GROSSETO ●

223

S1

Grosseto Azienda di
Promozione Turistica
Viale Monterosa 206 58100
Grosseto
Tel (0564) 454510
Fax (0564) 454606

Orbetello ●

The city of Grosseto is industrialized and of little interest to tourists, but the region's second city, Massa Marittima - which lies in the strange Colline Metallifere (metal-bearing hills) – is quite a different matter – an enchanting place. As for the inland hills, they are wild and little changed; little visited too: this is an area of Tuscany appreciated at present only by the *cognoscenti* – as reflected by the small number of acceptable hotels which we managed to find. One lies deep in the Maremma, once a maleria-infested marshland, now fertile farmland rich in wildlife, particularly wild boar. The others are on the coast, which is dedicated to Italian sun worshippers *en masse*, though the hotels' location, Punta Ala, is reserved for the Tuscan smart set.

332

Saturnia
● 161

Montemerano
● 160

74

● **Ansedonia**
160

Pisa

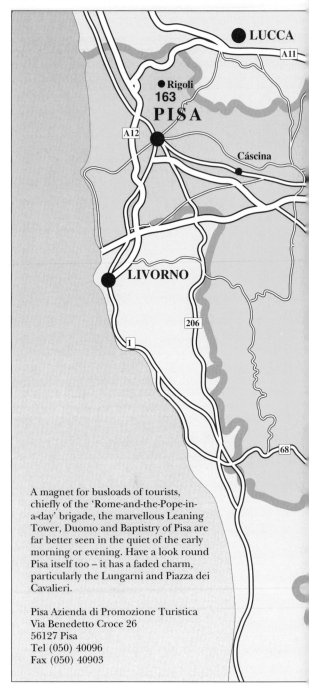

A magnet for busloads of tourists, chiefly of the 'Rome-and-the-Pope-in-a-day' brigade, the marvellous Leaning Tower, Duomo and Baptistry of Pisa are far better seen in the quiet of the early morning or evening. Have a look round Pisa itself too – it has a faded charm, particularly the Lungarni and Piazza dei Cavalieri.

Pisa Azienda di Promozione Turistica
Via Benedetto Croce 26
56127 Pisa
Tel (050) 40096
Fax (050) 40903

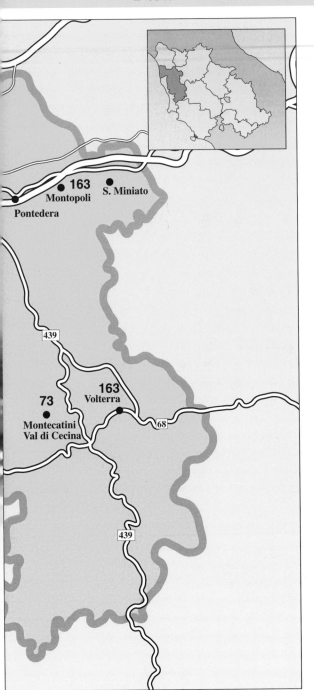

163
Montopoli ● S. Miniato

● Pontedera

439

73
Montecatini
Val di Cecina ●

163
Volterra ●

68

439

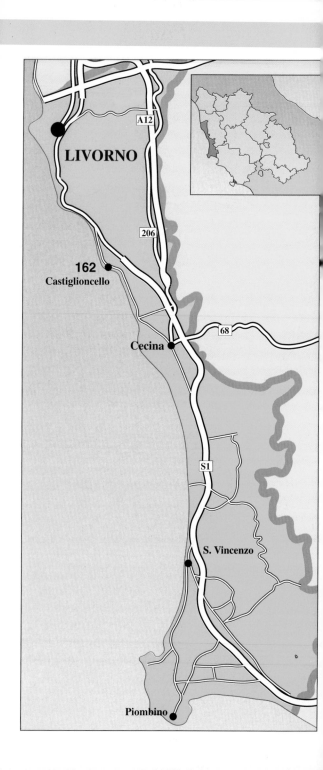

LIVORNO

A12

206

162
Castiglioncello

68

Cecina

S1

S. Vincenzo

Piombino

Arezzo

Mountain Hotel, Caprese Michelangelo

Fonte della Galletta

A winding climb through chestnut woods takes you up from the summer heat of the Tiber plain into the walkers' kingdom of the Alpe di Catinaia. At 800 m above sea level, the temperature here rarely reaches 30°C, even on the hottest July day.

The father of the present owners built this stone retreat some 30 years ago in a style that owes more to Switzerland than Tuscany. For most of the year (except weekends and August), it is a tranquil, almost forgotten place. This is its chief charm.

The modern bedrooms in the main building, refurbished in 1994, are small and rather anonymous, while the annexe rooms have been reburbished more recently. The beds are softly sprung, though the proprietor will place a board beneath the mattress if you prefer. Downstairs, the pine-tabled restaurant is anything but cosy. It does, however, offer a tempting range of local dishes according to season.

From the hotel, paths take you up through beech woods to the meadows of the Prate della Regina and the 1,400-m summit of Monte il Castello, with views of the Tiber and east to the Casentino. **Nearby** Michelangelo's birthplace at Caprese Michelangelo (6 km).

Alpe Faggetta,
Caprese Michelangelo, 52033
Arezzo
Tel & fax (0575) 793925/
793652
Location 6 km above Caprese
Michelangelo; ample car
parking.
Meals breakfast, lunch,
dinner
Prices rooms L; dinner
L40,000
Rooms 13 double in the hotel
& 6 in separate annexe,
3 singles, all with shower; all
rooms have heating, TV
Facilities restaurant, bar,
sitting-room; garden, lake
Credit cards AE, MC, V
Children accepted
Disabled access possible
Pets not accepted
Closed 6 Jan to May (except
weekends)
Languages English
Proprietors Berlicchi family

Arezzo

Country Villa, Castiglion Fiorentino

Villa Schiatti

Set among olive groves, this substantial Tuscan villa offers the space and simplicity of a family hotel with a number of apartments for longer-term guests. The Schiatti family built their two-towered villa between Castiglion Fiorentino and that most Tuscan of Tuscan hilltowns, Cortona, in the early years of the 19thC, but they lived here for barely a century before their line disappeared.

The present owners, the Bortot family, arrived in 1989 and set about restoring the villa with the minimum of interference to the original structure. Most of its stone and brick floors remain as they were, while the walls are whitewashed and its modest rooms are furnished with unobjectionable reproduction rustic furniture. The interior, however, lacks touches of thoughtful detail.

Signora Patrizia Bortot's quiet and friendly welcome – she speaks fluent English as well as German and French – and the reasonableness of the charges have helped to bring back an increasing number of guests each year. The evening meal, served at eight in the villa's rather impersonal dining-room, is simple and wholesome.

Nearby Castiglion Fiorentino (3 km); Cortona (8 km).

Località Montecchio, 131
Castiglion Fiorentino,
52043 Arezzo
Tel (0575) 651481
Fax (0575) 651482
Location 5 km S of Castiglion Fiorentino, 1 km above the SS71; with gardens and car parking
Meals breakfast, dinner
Prices rooms L
Rooms 9 double rooms with shower; three family apartments; all rooms have central heating, TV, phone
Facilities dining-room, bar, meeting room; terrace, garden, table tennis, swimming-pool
Credit cards AE, MC, V
Children welcome
Disabled access difficult
Pets accepted
Closed Jan
Languages English, French, German
Proprietors Bortot family

Arezzo

Agri Salotto

On the plain of Valdichiana, below Cortona clinging to its hillside, can be found a type of farmhouse unique in Tuscany. Constructed during the 18thC when the area was part of the Grand Duchy of Tuscany, they are known as *case leopoldiane*. On the ground floors were the stables and store-rooms; upstairs were the living quarters and, rising above the main roof, a pigeon-loft. Sadly, many of these have fallen into disrepair over the years, but the Bianchis have made a fine job of restoring one of the few remaining.

On the ground floor is a light and airy, U-shaped space occupied by the restaurant and the sitting area where guests take their *aperitivi* and coffee on large, comfortable sofas. The essential austerity of the Tuscan rustic style has been softened by antique mirrors and deep blue Chinese vases. Most of the apartments are upstairs, spacious and bright, stylishly furnished with a mixture of old and new pieces. Prices are reasonable and overnight stays are possible (subject to availability in high season). A garden and large swimming-pool are at the disposal of guests, and the tranquillity of the surrounding countryside will make you want to prolong your stay.
Nearby Cortona (10 km); Siena (54 km).

Loc. Burcinella 88,
Santa Caterina di Cortona,
52040 Arezzo
Tel (0575) 617417
Fax (0575) 617417
Location in own grounds;
ample car parking
Meals dinner,
Prices LL
Rooms 5 apartments (1 two-person, 2 four-person, 2 six-person), all with bath or shower, phone, TV, living-room, kitchen

Facilities sitting-room,
restaurant, laundry,
garden, swimming-pool
Smoking permitted
Credit cards not accepted
Children careful children only
Disabled one adapted
apartment
Pets not accepted
Closed 3 weeks in Jan
Languages English, French
Proprietors Silvana and
Giovanni Bianchi

Arezzo

Country villa hotel, Cortona

Il Falconiere

The plain surrounding Lake Trasimeno over which Il Falconiere looks was once the scene of some of Hannibal's fiercest battles against the Romans, and many of the local place-names refer to bones and blood. Nowadays the only carnage takes place on the A1 autostrada (the Sunny Motorway) but Il Falconiere is such a haven of civilized living that you will never realize that you are only twenty minutes away from one of Italy's riskiest tourist experiences.

Reached through quiet country lanes just outside Cortona, the main villa (built in the 17thC around an earlier fortified tower) is set in landscaped grounds of olives, rosemary hedges, fruit trees and roses, which also contain the old lemon house (now a top-class restaurant) and the still-functioning chapel with an adjoining suite. Meticulous attention has been given to every aspect of decoration and furnishing, from *trompe-l'oeil* number scrolls outside each room to the hand-embroidered window-hangings. Persian rugs rest easily on uneven, antique terracotta floors. In the pigeon-loft of the old tower, reached by a narrow, stone spiral staircase, is a small bedroom with an unsurpassed view of the Valdichiana.

Nearby Cortona (3 km); Arezzo (29 km); Lake Trasimeno (10 km).

Loc. San Martino, Cortona, 52044 Arezzo
Tel (0575) 612 679
Fax (0575) 612 927
Location just outside Cortona in its own grounds overlooking Valdichiana; ample parking
Meals breakfast, lunch, dinner
Prices LL-LLLL
Rooms 10 double, 2 suites; all with bath or shower, air-conditioning, minibar, phone, TV, safe
Facilities swimming-pool (May-Sep only), gardens, restaurant
Smoking permitted
Credit cards AE, DC, V
Children welcome
Disabled no special facilities
Pets yes but not in rooms
Closed 6 Jan to mid-Feb
Languages English, French, German
Proprietors Riccardo Baracchi and Silvia Regi

Arezzo

San Michele

It might sound like an easy matter to turn a fine Renaissance palace into a hotel of character, but we have seen too many examples of good buildings brutalised by excessive and unwanted luxury, over-modernization and an almost wilful blindness to the original style, not to be delighted when the job has been properly done.

The Hotel San Michele has not fluffed the opportunites offered by the former seat of the Etruscan Academy, but has steered a precise course between the twin dangers of unwarranted adventurousness and lame timidity. White plaster and stark beams are complemented with rich modern fabrics; sofas of the finest leather are strewn about terracotta floors that seem glazed with some rich wax. Carefully-placed lights emphasize the gracefully interlocking curves of the cortile. The common rooms are full of such stylish features as frescoed friezes and immense carved stone fireplaces.

The bedrooms are more modest in style, with wrought-iron beds and rustic antiques, and in need of refurbishment according to a recent report. Some of the more spacious ones have an extra mezzanine to provide separate sleeping and sitting areas.

Nearby Diocesan Museum, Arezzo (29 km); Perugia (51 km).

Via Guelfa 15, Cortona, 52044 Arezzo
Tel (0575) 604348
Fax (0575) 630147
Location 16th C. palazzo in middle of town; garage nearby
Meals breakfast only
Prices LLL
Rooms 40 double, all with bath or shower; TV, phone, minibar
Facilities garage, sitting-room, breakfast-room, conference-room
Smoking non-smoking area in breakfast-room
Credit cards AE, DC, MC, V
Children welcome
Disabled one suitable room
Pets small dogs
Closed 15 Jan-6 Mar
Languages English, French, German
Proprietor Paolo Alunno

Arezzo

Hilltop castle, Monte San Savino

Castello di Gargonza

A tree-lined road sweeps up the hill alongside the castle walls and brings you into the main square of this fortress-village, dominated by a stately crenellated tower where in more dangerous days lookouts surveyed the Valdichiana below for signs of approaching enemies. The village is as it was centuries ago, a jumble of stone houses connected by crooked paths. Traffic is not allowed in the castle area (except for loading and unloading baggage) and there is a hushed silent atmosphere which at night seems almost eerie – but don't let that put you off.

Most of the accommodation is given over to apartments in 19 picturesque houses, each with its own name, available for weekly rentals (occasionally for less), sleeping from two to seven persons. They make ideal choices for families. Overnight stays are available in the guest-house next to the reception. The rooms are simple.

At the bottom of the hill is the Torre di Gargonza restaurant of which we have mixed reports. The grounds have recently been improved and there is a new swimming-pool next door. Reports would be welcome.

Nearby Siena (35 km); Arezzo (25 km).

Gargonza, Monte San Savino, 52048 Arezzo
Tel (0575) 847021/22/23
Fax (0575) 847054
Location 8 km W of Monte San Savino, off the SS 73; car parking outside the castle
Meals breakfast, lunch, dinner
Prices LL-LLL
Rooms 6 double, 1 triple, all with bath or shower, phone; 25 self-catering apartments with 1 to 4 bedrooms

Facilities 4 sitting-rooms (2 for meetings), bar, restaurant, swimming-pool, bowls
Smoking permitted
Credit cards AE, DC, EC, MC, V **Children** welcome
Disabled not suitable
Pets small dogs
Closed 3 weeks in Nov and Jan **Languages** English, French, some German
Proprietor Conte Roberto Guicciardini

Firenze

Country hotel, Artimino

Paggeria Medicea

Villa Artimino, a Medici villa built when the family was at the height of its powers, stands high in the hills of the wine-producing district of Carmignano, west of Florence. Money from their banking activities and a sense of style that made them the greatest ever patrons of the arts combined to make this one of their most magnificent country residences. The villa is now a museum, but the former stables are an excellent hotel.

They certainly did their grooms well. Both sides of the long, low building are flanked by beautifully articulated loggias on to which most of the bedrooms open. The rooms themselves are spacious and shadily cool in summer; in other seasons, visitors may find that the loggia prevents enough light from getting in. Each has a large stone fireplace so that the roof, like the villa's beside, is cluttered with chimneys standing to attention like toy soldiers.

Downstairs, the stalls have been turned into breakfast-rooms and sitting areas full of comfortable couches, interesting books, old rugs and prints. The gardens look on to the city simmering on the sultry plain below and, even in July, catch a cool evening breeze.

Nearby Prato (15 km); Florence (24 km); Etruscan museum.

Viale Papa Giovanni XXIII, Artimino, 59015 Firenze
Tel (055) 871 8081
Fax (055) 871 8080
Location 24 km NW of Florence, with car parking
Meals breakfast, lunch, dinner
Prices LLL
Rooms 34 double, some with bath, most with shower; 3 single with shower; all have central heating, air-conditioning, minibar, TV, phone, radio; 32 apartments in Artimino village
Facilities breakfast-room, sitting-room, TV room, restaurant, 2 tennis-courts, jogging, swimming-pool, mountain bikes, laundry
Smoking permitted **Credit cards** AE, DC, MC, V
Children welcome **Disabled** some rooms accessible
Pets accepted **Closed** never
Languages English, French
Manager Alessandro Gualtieri

Firenze

Country guest-house, Barberino Val d'Elsa

Il Paretaio

A great address for those interested in horse-riding but not to be dismissed by travellers in search of the country life. Strategically located between Florence and Siena, in hilly surroundings, Il Paretaio is a 17thC stone-built farmhouse on its own large estate.

The accommodation is simple but attractive. The ground-floor entrance and sitting area was originally a work-room, and still retains the old stone paving. A huge brick arch spans the central space and brick-vaulting contrasts with the plain white walls. Upstairs, the rustic style is continued in the exposed-beam ceilings and worn terracotta floors.

The dining-room is particularly attractive with its larch-wood table, ten feet long, where communal meals are served, and a huge open fireplace. Most of the bedrooms are off this room, with country furniture and equestrian prints. The most attractive bedroom is in the dovecot, a mini-tower at the top of the house with pretty little arched windows on three sides looking on to the rolling landscape.

Outside is a riding arena, and a swimming-pool.

Nearby Florence (33 km); San Gimignano (21 km); Siena (34 km).

Loc. San Filippo, Barberino Val d'Elsa, 50021 Firenze
Tel (055) 8059218
Fax (055) 8059231
Location 3 km S of Barberino Val d'Elsa
Meals breakfast, dinner
Prices L
Rooms 6 double; two apartments for 4-5 people; reductions for children
Facilities garden, swimming-pool, horse-riding, (all standards and all ages), mountain bikes
Smoking allowed (except in dining-room)
Credit cards not accepted
Children welcome
Disabled no special facilities
Pets accepted
Closed never
Languages English, French
Proprietors Giovanni and Cristina de Marchi

Firenze

Osteria del Vicario

The modern development of Certaldo has led to the growth of a town so ugly as to be almost on a par with Poggibonsi, making for a formidably discouraging approach to the Osteria del Vicario. But persevere and follow the directions for 'Certaldo Alto'. What has saved the old town and made it a world apart from its unattractive sibling is its location on its own hill. Unusually for Tuscany, which is characterized by a heavy usage of local grey stone, Certaldo Alto is built almost entirely of polytonal brick that changes colour according to the light, in step with the seasons and the time of day.

In the centre of the old town, next to the Palazzo del Prefettorio, stands the Osteria del Vicario, which was taken over a few years ago by owners eager to maintain the establishment's reputation as a restaurant, and who extended it to include overnight accommodation. Decoration is standard rustic, set in well-proportioned interiors that preserve the original features of the old town-house. At the back is a secluded pebble-garden with a pergola where one can breakfast or dine while taking in a long Tuscan view. Not sophisticated but good value.

Nearby Florence (41 km); San Gimignano (14 km); Siena (42 km).

Via Rivellino 3, Certaldo Alto,
50052 Firenze
Tel (055) 668228
Fax (055) 668228
Location in the old part
of Certaldo ('alto'); car
parking nearby
Meals breakfast, lunch,
dinner
Prices LL
Rooms 2 single, 9 double, all
with bath or shower, TV
Smoking permitted

Credit cards AE, DC, EC, V
Children welcome
Disabled no special facilities
Pets accepted
Closed last 3 weeks of Jan
(restaurant shut on Wed)
Languages English, French
Proprietors Sara Conforti
and Claudio Borchi

Firenze

Farm guest-house, Cortine

La Chiara di Prumiano

A useful base for families who want to mix touring with just enjoying the Tuscan countryside. The simply furnished 17thC farmhouse, reached by a long, unsurfaced road, offers great views. The interiors are light and airy, but definitely modest in style, and will appeal to visitors who are looking for an honest country holiday rather than flashy luxury. The owners of La Chiara di Prumiano, who moved here from Milan some years ago, enjoy an informal and often slightly 'alternative' style of life that gives the place a laid-back atmosphere. They follow the macrobiotic approach to agriculture, and you can be sure that the food served in the dining-room is of genuine quality – although those fond of *bistecca alla fiorentina* might regret the vegetarian slant.

Plenty of outdoor activities await the energetic: horses either for trekking or for use in the farm's own riding-ground; a swimming-pool; a volleyball court; and the surrounding countryside for walks. Rather too close to the Siena-Florence dual carriageway for some, La Chiara's central location, however, also makes it a convenient base from which to visit many of Tuscany's *città d'arte*.

Nearby Siena (40 km); San Gimignano (25 km).

Loc. Prumiano, Strada di
Cortine 12,
Barberino Val d'Elsa, 50021
Firenze
Tel (055) 8075727
Fax (055) 8075678
Location approach best made
on road from S. Donato (not
Barberino); own grounds; car
parking
Meals breakfast, lunch,
dinner
Prices L-LL (DB&B)
Rooms 15 double, 9 with bath

or shower
Facilities sitting-room,
restaurant, garden,
swimming-pool, volley-ball,
horse-riding
Smoking permitted
Credit cards MC, EC, V
Children welcome
Disabled some adapted rooms
Pets accepted
Closed 2 weeks at Christmas
Languages English, French,
Spanish
Proprietor Gaia Mezzadri

Firenze

Country villa, Fiesole

Bencista

It is not difficult to see why the Bencista is an old favourite with a regular clientèle. By no means a luxurious place, it is all the same full of individual character and offers excellent value for its location on the chic hillside of Fiesole, with panoramic views over the red roofs of the city dominated by Brunelleschi's incomparable dome. Cooler in the evening than sultry Florence, surrounded by complete peace and quiet, you can still be in the centre in half an hour (a regular bus service has a stop five minutes away). Nearby are some excellent restaurants and walks.

The building, which was once a monastery, is no architectural gem, though it is full of character. Three sitting-rooms surround the entrance area, each decorated in a different style: striped couches, gilt-framed paintings and prints and a grand-piano contribute to a distinctly Edwardian feel. The dining-room is like an old-fashioned *trattoria* with a view over the gardens. Half-board is obligatory: there is no choice at dinner and we have heard differing reports about the food. Bedrooms are comfortable rather than stylish. Some have their own terraces.

Nearby Florence (8 km); Fiesole (2 km).

Via B. da Maiano 4, Fiesole, 50014 Firenze
Tel (055) 59163
Fax (055) 59163
Location 8 km N of Florence on the hill of Fiesole, 2.5 km S of the town; in its own grounds, ample car parking
Meals breakfast, lunch, dinner
Prices LLL (DB&B)
Rooms 29 double, 13 single, all except 12 with bath or shower, central-heating, phone
Facilities sitting-rooms, dining-room, terrace, garden; no TV **Smoking** not allowed except in one sitting-room
Credit cards not accepted
Children welcome
Disabled no special facilities
Pets not accepted **Closed** never **Languages** English, French, German
Proprietor Simone Simoni

Firenze

Country guest-house, Fiesole

Il Trebbiolo

Small, intimate and elegant, Il Trebbiolo stands on a quiet hillside just north of Fiesole, surrounded by acres of vines and olives. A large gravel terrace in front of the house, shaded by spindly pines, looks on to the open countryside towards the Mugello valley.

The villa, a simple ochre-coloured building with green shutters, is flanked by two elegant, arched loggias. Extreme care and taste has been spent decorating and furnishing the interiors with fine antiques and modern Tuscan art, perfectly assembled in the light, well-proportioned rooms. Subdued lighting and an imaginative combination of colours contribute to a soothing overall effect.

The bedrooms maintain the high standards of the public rooms, and each one takes a different colour as its theme. Here too you will find the books that are so much a part of this cultured household (the owner, Carla Rossi, is a director of a well-known Florentine book shop), and comfortable armchairs in which to read them. The bathrooms, with their green marble floors and modern tiling, live up to expectations. All in all, one of the finest guest-houses in the Florence area.

Nearby Fiesole (7 km); Florence (16 km).

8 Via del Trebbiolo, Molin del Piano, Fiesole, 50060 Firenze
Tel (055) 8300098
Fax (055) 8300583
Location 10 km NE of Florence in its own grounds; car parking
Meals breakfast, dinner
Prices LL-LLL
Rooms 6 double, 2 single, 1 suite, all with bath or shower, phone, TV, minibar

Facilities sitting-room, restaurant; garden
Smoking permitted
Credit cards AE, EC, MC, V
Children welcome
Disabled no special facilities
Pets dogs not accepted
Closed mid-Jan to mid-Feb; Aug
Languages English, French
Proprietor Carla Rossi

TUSCANY

Firenze

Converted monastery, Fiesole

Villa San Michele

A hotel so expensive that even its cheapest single rooms, which are rather small, lie well outside the price range represented by our symbols: one of the better suites will cost you over two million lire, enough to pay dinner for ten people at Florence's finest restaurant. At these prices one expects transcendent perfection, but we have the feeling that part of the frisson of staying at San Michele is having paid so much in the first place.

Cost aside, the hotel is undoubtedly among the finest in the guide, both for its location, and for the character of its buildings, whose post-war restoration has been successful in removing some insensitive 19thC embellishments and repairing bomb damage. The dignified façade with its porticoed loggia is based on a design attributed to Michaelangelo, and once you pass through the doors you have the odd sensation of checking-in to a former church. Antiques, acquired without heed of expense, abound, although there is also some modern furniture. Bedrooms in the new annex have less character than those in the original building. The chic restaurant serves meals on a lovely, covered lemon terrace.

Nearby Florence (6 km); Fiesole (1 km).

Via di Doccia 4, Fiesole, 50014 Firenze
Tel (055) 595451
Fax (055) 598734
Location just below Fiesole, on hill-side overlooking Florence; own grounds with car parking
Meals breakfast, lunch, dinner
Prices LLLL+
Rooms 25 double, 15 suites, all with bath and shower, phone, TV, heating, air-conditioning
Facilities sitting-rooms, bar, restaurant, terrace, swimming-pool, private city bus shuttle **Smoking** allowed
Credit cards AE, DC, EC, MC, V **Children** welcome
Disabled one suitable room
Pets small dogs only (not in restaurant or near pool)
Closed end-Nov to mid-Mar
Languages English, French, German, Spanish
Manager Maurizio Saccani

Firenze

Town guest-house, Florence

Annalena

One of Florence's traditional *pensioni,* still very much in the old style, with a regular clientèle. The Annalena is located opposite the Boboli gardens (the famous park laid out by Medici dukes) and many of the rooms look out on to a horticultural centre next door. Luckily, none of them has windows on the busy Via Romana.

The *palazzo* is said to be 15thC, belonging at one point to a young noblewoman, Annalena, whose tragic love story and early widowhood led her to withdraw from the world and give over her property as a place of retirement for other young widows. Since then, the *palazzo* has been offering hospitality of one sort or another, and during the war gave refuge to many foreigners in flight from Mussolini's police.

The tradition of hospitality continues to this day, and while the Annalena is no luxury hotel, it offers solid comforts not without hints of style at reasonable prices, with an owner attentive to his guests' needs. A huge salon now serves as reception, sitting-room, breakfast-room and bar. Bedrooms vary in size and bathrooms are acceptable.

Nearby Palazzo Pitti, Ponte Vecchio, Palazzo Vecchio, Uffizi.

Via Romana 34, 50125
Firenze
Tel (055) 222402/3
Fax (055) 222402/3
Location 3 minutes' walk
from Palazzo Pitti on S side of
river; pay car parking nearby
(20,000 lire approx.)
Meals breakfast
Prices LL-LLL
Rooms 4 single, 16 double,
all with bath or shower,
phone, TV

Facilities sitting-room, bar
breakfast-room, terrace
Smoking allowed
Credit cards AE, DC, EC, MC,
V
Children welcome
Disabled no special facilities
Pets accepted
Closed never
Languages English, French,
Greek
Proprietor Claudio Salvestrini

Town hotel, Florence

Guelfo Bianco

By no means one of Florence's great hotels, but a sound choice for travellers looking for comfort and a central location at reasonable prices. This and the friendly attitude of the owners, eager to assist their guests with tips on restaurants and planning their stay in Florence, makes Il Guelfo Bianco an address worth noting.

Via Cavour, where the hotel is situated, is one of the city's busier streets, running from Piazza del Duomo to Piazza San Marco. Luckily, the rooms are sound-proofed and air-conditioned (and both are necessary during the summer) but if you are a light sleeper, make sure to ask for a room on the quiet side.

The building is a 17thC *palazzo* with an entrance on the street that brings you into a small narrow foyer containing the bar and reception. Restoration has left intact the character of the quiet, subdued interiors. Bedrooms are tasteful and modern, many with their own sitting areas. Original paintings add a note of style, especially in the breakfast-room, a light, spacious area where a buffet of fruits, cereals, salamis and cheeses will start your day well.

Nearby Palazzo Medici-Riccardi, San Lorenzo church and market, San Marco, Duomo, Baptistery, Accademia.

Via Cavour 29, 50129 Firenze
Tel (055) 288330
Fax (055) 295203
Location in centre of town, 2 minutes' walk N of the Duomo, by the Palazzo Medici-Riccardi; pay car parking nearby
Meals breakfast
Prices LL-LLL
Rooms 13 single, 26 double, all with bath or shower, phone, TV, minibar, safe, air-conditioning

Facilities sitting-room, bar, breakfast-room
Credit cards AE, EC, MC, V
Children welcome; family rooms available
Disabled two adapted rooms
Pets not accepted
Closed never
Languages English, French, German, Spanish
Proprietor Luisa Ginti

Firenze

Helvetia & Bristol

The Helvetia was originally a Swiss-owned hotel right in the centre of Florence which added the name Bristol to attract 19thC British travellers. After 1945, it gradually fell into decay until new management took it over and began restoration in 1987, sparing no expense in their imaginative recreation of a 19thC luxury hotel.

Those with classical tastes, used to the stark simplicity of the Tuscan style, may find the results cloying and indigestible, but others will enjoy the rich colour schemes and heavy, dark antiques. The restaurant is undeniably elegant and hung with two amazing Art Nouveau lamps shaped like shells and rocks. The least overwhelming room is a 1920s winter-garden, full of handsome cane furniture and potted palms, with a green-tinted glass ceiling. The bedrooms are, if anything, even more ornate than the public rooms, with heavy fabrics used on walls, windows and beds alike. Antiques, Venetian mirrors and chandeliers add to the opulence. One of the finest features of the hotel is its extensive collection of prints and pictures, including a lovely 19thC copy of a Raphael Madonna. Staff and service are smooth and professional.

Nearby Ponte Vecchio, Uffizi, Palazzo Vecchio, Palazzo Pitti.

Via dei Pescioni 2, 50123
Firenze
Tel (055) 287814
Fax (055) 288353
Location in the centre of
town, opposite Palazzo
Strozzi, W of Piazza
Repubblica; pay car parking
nearby
Meals breakfast, lunch,
dinner
Prices LLLL
Rooms 9 single, 20 double, 5
suites, all with bath or
shower, phone, TV, minibar,
air-conditioning
Facilities sitting-rooms,
restaurant, bar, winter-garden
Smoking some non-smoking
areas
Credit cards AE, DC, EC,
MC, V
Children welcome
Disabled some facilities
Pets small dogs **Closed** never
Languages English, French,
German, Spanish
Manager Petro Panelli

Firenze

Town guest-house, Florence

Hermitage

A hotel you are hardly likely to stumble across, despite its central location next to the Ponte Vecchio on the north side of the Arno. A discreetly placed entrance in a small alley-way, opposite the porticos supporting Vasari's corridor, admits you to a lift taking you up five floors to the reception and its friendly, international staff.

The Hermitage is like a *cappuccino*: the best bits are on top and matters become more mundane as you descend. The roof terrace, filled with flowers in terracotta pots, shade provided by a pergola, commands unrivalled views of the city. Sitting there at breakfast, you can plan the day's excursions almost without the aid of a map. In case of bad weather, there is a light and airy breakfast-room on the fifth floor with a covered veranda. Next door is the sitting-room (and bar) looking directly on to the Ponte Vecchio and the Oltrarno, with comfortable couches. Bedrooms combine fairly successfully modern and old-fashioned furniture. After the Uffizi bombing in 1993, the streets around were banned to traffic, so noise is not a problem – assisted by the judicious, although not always sufficient, double-glazing on the busier riverside aspect.

Nearby Ponte Vecchio, Uffizi, Palazzo Vecchio, Palazzo Pitti, Duomo.

Vicolo Marzio 1, Piazza del Pesce, 50122 Firenze
Tel (055) 287216
Fax (055) 212208
E-mail florence@hermitagehotel.com
Website http://www.hermitagehotel.com
Location right beside the Ponte Vecchio; private pay car parking nearby
Meals breakfast
Prices LLLL
Rooms 3 single, 28 double, all with bath and/or shower; all rooms have central heating, air-conditioning phone, satellite TV
Facilities sitting-room, bar, breakfast-room, roof-garden
Smoking allowed **Credit cards** V **Children** welcome
Disabled not suitable
Pets accepted **Closed** never
Languages English, German, Portuguese **Proprietor** Vincenzo Scarcelli

Firenze

Town hotel, Florence

J and J

This highly individual hotel in a former convent of the 16thC is to be found, off the usual tourist routes, in a residential part of the old city centre. However, it is still convenient for visiting all the obligatory Florentine museums, with the advantage of peace and quiet when you get back to the hotel in the evening.

Perhaps it was the owner's training as an architect that gave him the confidence to combine old and new so strikingly in the decoration and furnishings. The building is, in fact, two, separated by a terracotta-paved cloister where breakfast is served during the summer months. In front of this, is a lovely light room with painted wicker furniture and a decorated vaulted ceiling, separated from the cloister only by the glassed-in arches. The sitting-room next door combines original features with pale modern furniture and mellow lighting.

Some of the bedrooms are enormous, possibly because they used to be studio flats, and could sleep a family of four in comfort. Each one is different in style, furnished with antiques and hand-woven fabrics. The character of the building does not allow for a lift.
Nearby Santa Croce, San Marco, Santissima Annunziata.

Via di Mezzo 20, 50121 Firenze
Tel (055) 240951
Fax (055) 240282
Location a few minutes' walk E of the Duomo
Meals breakfast only
Prices LLLL
Rooms 18 double, two family rooms, all with bath or shower, phone, TV, minibar, air-conditioning
Facilities sitting-room, breakfast-room, courtyard
Smoking permitted
Credit cards AE, DC, EC, MC, V
Children welcome
Disabled no special facilities
Pets not accepted
Closed never
Languages English, French, German
Proprietor James Cavagnari

Firenze

Town hotel, Florence

Loggiato dei Serviti

noice of accommodation in the centre of Florence always pre-
nts the visitor with a dilemma: stylish establishments cost so much
u feel that you should spend the entire day indoors, getting value
r your money, while budget *pensioni* have the opposite effect. In
ur first edition, we said that none strikes the balance so well as
oggiato dei Serviti. Now, sadly, we have to qualify this by the fact
at the piazza where the hotel stands is frequented by drug
dicts. That aside, the Piazza Santissima Annunziata is Florence's
ost beautiful square. New, strict traffic regulations mean that the
azza no longer looks like a car park (however, it is difficult to get
 the Loggiato by car) and one can now enjoy the full beauty of its
egant colonnades and equestrian statue.

The hotel is on the side opposite Brunelleschi's Ospedale degli
nocenti, underneath a portico decorated with ceramic medal-
ons by della Robbia. The interior is cool and restrained; rooms
e furnished with antiques and well-chosen modern pieces, some
oking on to the piazza, others on to gardens behind. The pleas-
t ground-floor breakfast-room has softly playing opera.

earby SS. Annunziato and San Marco; Accademia museum.

Piazza SS. Annunziata 3,
50122 Firenze
Tel (055) 289 592/3/4
Fax (055) 289595
Location five minute's walk
from the Duomo, in quiet
piazza; pay car parking in
garage nearby
Meals breakfast
Prices LL-LLLL
Rooms 19 double, 6 single,
4 suites, all with bath or
shower, phone, TV, radio,
safe, air-conditioning
Facilities breakfast-room, bar
Smoking permitted
Credit cards AE, DC, EC, MC,
V
Children welcome
Disabled not suitable
Pets please check first
Closed never
Languages English, French
Proprietor Rodolfo Buttini
Gattai

Firenze

Town hotel, Florence

Monna Lisa

The entrance is as discreet as the hotel itself: at the back of a cc
ered area opening into the *palazzo* from Borgo Pinti, used
bygone days for parking the *padrone's* horse-and-carriage, is a sm
door leading into this intriguing hotel.

A maze of rooms occupies the ground floor with Doric a■
Corinthian columns of *pietra serena* supporting heavy, decorat■
wooden ceilings. Light floods in from the back through leaded w■
dows that give on to the garden. Old terracotta floors, dark a■
shiny from centuries of wax polish, lead the eye easily from o■
room to another. The family's collection of paintings and scu■
ture (including the original model for Giambologna's *Rape of* ■
Sabine Women) give a pleasant cluttered air to the public areas.

The garden is a definite plus in this claustrophobic city, so sh■
of quiet, shady places in which to sit. Breakfast can be taken here
fine weather. Some of the bedrooms, in heavy, ornate style, ha■
small terraces overlooking this delightful green haven.

One caution: we've had reports that reception can be somewh■
cool. Reports from readers would be appreciated.

Nearby Cathedral, Santissima Annunziata, San Marco, Santa Croc■

Borgo Pinti 27, 50121 Firenze
Tel (055) 2479751
Fax (055) 2479755
Location 5 minutes' walk E of
the Duomo; pay car parking
nearby
Meals breakfast
Prices LLL-LLLL
Rooms 30 double, 5 single,
all with bath or shower,
phone, TV, minibar, heating,
air-conditioning
Facilities sitting-rooms, bar,

garden, private parking in Vi■
della Pergola
Smoking permitted
Credit cards AE, DC, EC, MC
V
Children welcome
Disabled one adapted room
Pets accepted
Closed never
Languages English, French,
German
Manager Agostino Cona

TUSCANY

Firenze

Town guest-house, Florence

Morandi alla Crocetta

Morandi alla Crocetta, a family-run *pensione* occupying an apartment in the university part of town in a road leading to Piazza
Santissima Annunziata. The entrance looks like any other on the
street, without any neon signs, and you must ring a bell to be
admitted. Reserve and discretion are the hallmarks here.

Quiet, tasteful interiors greet visitors in the second-floor apartment. The polished wooden floors, with strategically placed oriental carpets, echo the beamed ceilings and their decorated corbels.
Architectural details are picked out in brick, and the white walls
carry only a very few paintings and portraits. There is a small, intimate breakfast-room. All is impeccably maintained.

The bedrooms, quiet and comfortable, are furnished with
antiques and some well-chosen modern pieces. Two of them have
small terraces opening on to a small garden and another has the
remains of 17thC frescoes depicting the life and works of Sister
Domenica del Paradiso, founder of the original convent.
Bathrooms are small but of a high standard. An ideal choice for visitors who need to recover from Florence's stressful centre.

Nearby Santissima Annunziata, San Marco, Baptistry, Duomo.

Via Laura 50, 50121 Firenze
Tel (055) 2344747
Fax (055) 2480954
Location in a quiet street, a
few minutes' walk N of the
Duomo; pay car parking
nearby
Meals breakfast
Prices LL
Rooms 4 double, 2 single, 4
family rooms, all with bath or
shower, phone, TV, minibar,
safe, central heating, air-
conditioning, hairdrier

Facilities sitting-room,
breakfast-room, bar
Smoking allowed
Credit cards AE, DC, EC, MC,
V
Children welcome
Disabled no special facilities
Pets well-behaved dogs
accepted
Closed never
Languages English, French,
German
Proprietor Kathleen Doyle
Antuono and family

53

Firenze

Town hotel, Florence

Regency

Slightly outside the city's historic centre, Piazza d'Azeglio is a larg
19thC square with villas built for high government officials whe
Florence briefly served as Italy's capital. Compared to the centre c
town, the square is peaceful, and Florence's small size makes it eas
to reach most of the main monuments from here on foot.

The Regency is decorated in a plush, opulent style appropriat
to the prices being charged. It did strike us, on occasion, that
lighter touch would have been welcome: attention is taken awa
from some fine pieces of furniture by the rich-coloured, patterne
carpets. In some of the bedrooms, the use of clashing fabrics crea
ed a fussy effect. The restaurant shows a more restrained hand
with stained-glass doors and subdued wooden panelling.

One of the most pleasant features of the Regency is the larg
garden behind the main villa (leading to the annex, which house
some of the other bedrooms). Cool and shady, anyone who ha
spent a tough day in the heat and pollution of central Florence wi
enjoy its soothing qualities. The breakfast-room, separated fror
the garden by glass walls, shares some of its peaceful atmosphere.
Nearby San Marco, Santa Croce, Duomo, Santissima Annunziata.

Piazza Massimo d'Azeglio 3,
50121 Firenze
Tel (055) 245247, 2342936
Fax (055) 2346935
Location 10 minutes' walk E
of the Duomo; pay car park-
ing nearby
Meals breakfast, lunch,
dinner
Prices LLL-LLLL
Rooms 30 double, 5 suites, all
with bath or shower, phone,
TV, safe, air-conditioning
Facilities sitting-room, bar,

breakfast-room, restaurant,
garden
Smoking some non-smoking
areas
Credit cards AE, DC, EC, MC,
V
Children welcome
Disabled no special facilities
Pets not in public rooms
Closed never
Languages English, French,
German
Proprietor Pietro Panelli

Firenze

Town guest-house, Florence

Tornabuoni Beacci

One could not ask for more in terms of location. Via Tornabuoni is one of Florence's most elegant and central shopping streets, where leading designers such as Gucci, Ferragamo and Ferré have their stores and within easy walking distance are all the main sights of the city. Yet its position on the fourth and fifth floors in the 15thC Palazzo Minerbetti Strozzi, at one corner of Piazza Santa Trinita, makes it a haven from Florence's crowded, noisy streets.

The *pensione* has a turn-of-the-century atmosphere; fans of E.M. Forster's A Room With A View will find this a close approximation to the Edwardian guest-house described in the novel. Many of the rooms have views, but none so fine as the roof-top terrace, with its plants and pergola, which looks over the city to the towers and villas of the Bellosguardo hill. Even in the hot, still days of July and August, you may catch a refreshing breeze here.

The decoration and furnishings are old-fashioned but well-maintained, like the house of a maiden aunt. Parquet floors and plain-covered sofas are much in evidence. Rooms vary – some are quite poky – but new management has been making improvements.
Nearby Santa Trinita, Ponte Vecchio, Palazzo della Signoria, Uffizi.

Via Tornabuoni 3, 50123
Firenze
Tel (055) 212645, 268377
Fax (055) 283594
Location in centre of town;
car parking in private garage
nearby (40,000 lire per day)
Meals breakfast, dinner,
snacks (in summer)
Prices LL-LLL
Rooms 8 single, 20 double,
all with bath or shower,
phone, TV, minibar, air-
conditioning

Facilities sitting-room,
restaurant, roof-terrace
Smoking allowed
Credit cards AE, DC, EC,
MC, V
Children welcome
Disabled difficult
Pets small dogs only
Closed never
Languages English, French,
German, Spanish
Proprietor Francesco Bechi

Firenze

Country villa, Florence

Torre di Bellosguardo

Everybody has heard of the hillside of Fiesole, north of Florence, site of the original Etruscan settlement in the area. Less well known, on the southern edge of the city, is the hill of Bellosguardo ('lovely view' in Italian), more discreet in atmosphere and without a busy town to attract trippers. What *will* draw visitors, however, is this fine hotel – close enough to Florence for easy access but far away enough to guarantee enjoyment of Tuscany's countryside.

As the name suggests, a tower stands at the heart of this 16thC villa, built originally for defence and then surrounded by the trappings of civilization as time passed by. Extraordinary care has been taken to restore the buildings to their former glory after years of abuse as a school in the post-war period. Spacious rooms with painted wood or vaulted ceilings, frescoed walls and the antiques appropriate to the setting create an atmosphere of character and distinction. No two bedrooms are alike and we saw only one (with a skylight rather than a window) that we thought less than admirable. Well-tended gardens filled with flowers, cypresses and magnolias boast a turquoise pool and city views.

Nearby Palazzo Pitti, Boboli gardens and other Florence sights.

Via Roti Michelozzi 2
50124 Firenze
Tel (055) 2298145
Fax (055) 229008
Location on the hill of Bellosguardo, just S of the city; car parking
Meals breakfast, lunch
Prices LLL-LLLL; breakfast L30,000
Rooms 8 double, 2 single, 6 suites, all with bath; all rooms have phone and central heating; 5 have
air-conditioning
Facilities sitting-rooms, breakfast-room, bar, garden, swimming-pool
Smoking allowed
Credit cards AE, EC, MC, V
Children welcome
Disabled no special facilities
Pets accepted
Closed never
Languages English, German, French
Proprietor Giovanni Franchetti

Firenze

Town hotel, Florence

Villa Azalee

onvenient for the station but slightly remote from the monumental
istrict (about 15 minutes by foot) Villa Azalee will appeal to visitors
ho prefer family-run hotels with some style to larger more luxuri-
us operations. And by the standards of most hotels in Florence,
rices are very reasonable. The hotel consists of two buildings: the
riginal 19thC villa and, across the garden, a new annexe, full of the
otted azaleas that give the place its name.

A highly individual style has been used in the decoration and fur-
iture: some will find the results delightful, others excessively whim-
cal. Pastel colours, frilly canopies and matching curtains and bed-
overs characterize the bedrooms. They are all air-conditioned, with
ootless, new bathrooms. Public rooms are more restrained with an
nteresting collection of the family's paintings. Breakfast is served
ither in your room or in the garden (somewhat noisy) or in a sepa-
ate breakfast-room.

One of the drawbacks of the hotel is its location on the *viali* (the
usy traffic arteries circling Florence). Sound proofing has been
sed, but rooms in the annexe, or overlooking the garden are best.
Nearby Santa Maria Novella, Ognissanti, San Lorenzo, Duomo.

Viale Fratelli Rosselli 44,
50123 Firenze
Tel (055) 214242
Fax (055) 268264
Location a few minutes' walk
W of the main station,
towards Porta al Prato; pay
car parking nearby (30,000
lire per day, approx.)
Meals breakfast
Prices LL-LLL
Rooms 2 single, 22 double,
all with bath or shower, air-

conditioning, TV, phone, TV,
minibar
Facilities sitting-room, bar,
garden
Smoking permitted
Credit cards AE, DC, EC, MC,
V
Children welcome
Disabled no special facilities
Pets please check first
Closed never
Languages English, French
Proprietor Ornella Brizzi

Firenze

Farm guest-house, Giogoli

Il Milione

In many ways an ideal location for those who like to combine ci
tourism with a country retreat. Il Milione is theoretically with
Florence's city limits, but you could just as well be in deepe
Tuscany. Convenient access to the *autostrada* brings Siena, Sa
Gimignano, Pisa, Lucca and Arezzo all within easy driving distanc
Nearby is the famous Certosa di Galluzzo. Yet Il Milione has ever
thing that a farm should have: vines, olives and honey, fresh eg
and vegetables, and acres of countryside to roam in. A swimmin
pool and a small lake are added attractions.

The eccentric name originates with Signora Husy's husbar
(now, alas, dead) Guscelli Brandimarte, a silversmith who, when I
wanted to buy the farm, borrowed a million lire from each of h
friends, repaying them with examples of his own workmanship. H
irrepressible spirit lives on at Il Milione in the sculptures that a
scattered throughout the gardens and in the silver place-settings
the dining-table. Rooms and apartments are spread througho
the farm's buildings. Booking ahead is essential. One of the be
bargains in the Florence area.

Nearby Florence (8 km); Siena (60 km).

Loc. Galluzzo, Via di Giogoli
14, 50124 Firenze
Tel (055) 2048713
Fax (055) 2048046
Location 8 km S of city
centre, in own grounds; car
parking
Meals self-catering, dinner on
request; fresh farm breakfast
ingredients supplied
Prices L-LL (DB&B)
Rooms 2 two-person
apartments, 5 four-person
apartments, all with bath or

shower, phone, TV; 3-day
minimum stay
Facilities sitting-room, dining-
room, garden, swimming-
pool, bowls, horse-riding
Smoking allowed
Credit cards not accepted
Children welcome
Disabled no special facilities
Pets not accepted
Closed never
Languages English, German,
French
Proprietor Jessica Husy

Firenze

Castello di Uzzano

Originally a 12thC castle which the additions of centuries have converted to an elegant and civilized country villa, surrounded on its hilltop by stately cypresses and umbrella pines. Adjacent to the villa is a delightful ornamental garden with geometrically laid out box hedges, battered old statues and terracotta urns filled with flowers. On the other side is a formal terrace which is neatly compartmented by gravel paths and weathered stone balustrades.

The apartments surround a courtyard to which the graceful loggia of the castle forms a backdrop. A great deal of imagination and flair has been put into their restoration and decoration. Each has been individually furnished with interesting antiques and fine old prints and paintings of a higher standard than one normally finds in this type of place.

Smart kitchens have been unobtrusively incorporated, but if you prefer to eat out, there are many excellent restaurants in the area.

Undeniably aristocratic, indisputably historical, Castello di Uzzano enables guests to relish an oasis of civilized living.
Nearby Florence (30 km); Siena (45 km).

Via Uzzano 5, Greve in Chianti, 50022 Firenze
Tel (055) 854032
Fax (055) 854375
Location 1 km N of Greve in own grounds; ample car parking
Meals none
Prices L-LL; one-week minimum stay
Rooms 6 fully equipped apartments for 2 to 4 persons
Facilities gardens, bikes

Smoking permitted
Credit cards EC, MC, V
Children welcome
Disabled no special facilities
Pets please check first
Closed never
Languages English, French, German
Proprietor Marion de Jacobert

Firenze

Converted castle, Greve in Chianti

Castello Vicchiomaggio

Here is a classic Chianti setting: a hilltop castle, complete with tower, overlooking a landscape of vine, olive and cypress. A winding white track leads you to the castle from the Chiantigiana, the main road through the heart of this famous wine region. And wine is the business of the Vicchiomaggio estate, which supplies supermarkets and shops all over Europe.

The castle dates back to the 10thC, but it was much embellished during the Renaissance. It's impressive, baronial and rather austere, perhaps impersonal. Formerly it was a finishing school for young ladies. The rooms in the self-catering apartments (small kitchen and dining area in each) are cavernous rather than cosy, but reasonably comfortable. Furnishings are mostly antique, although there are some inappropriate modern sofas. We liked a lower-ceilinged room under the roof, with antique bedstead.

The vast main dining-room has vaulted ceilings, a stone fireplace and a Tuscan menu. There are weekly wine tastings in the estate cellars. Outside, well-kept terraces and walks afford beautiful views, although a sense of tranquillity can at times be hard to come by.
Nearby Greve (5 km); Florence (19 km); Siena (38 km).

Greve in Chianti, 50022
Florence
Tel (055) 854079
Fax (055) 853911
Location off the SS222 ,
4 km N of Greve, set in its
own extensive grounds, with
ample car parking
Meals breakfast, lunch,
dinner
Prices L-LL
Rooms 7 double-bedded
mini-apartments, for two,
four and six people, all with
bath, kitchen and central
heating **Facilities** restaurant,
terraces, garden, walks
Credit cards MC, V
Children welcome
Disabled no special facilities
Pets welcome if small
Closed restaurant only, Jan to
Mar (except weekends)
Languages English, German,
French
Proprietor John Matta

Firenze

Country villa, Greve in Chianti

Villa di Vignamaggio

Chianti has more than its share of hill-top villas and castles, now posing as hotels, or, as in this case, self-catering *(agriturismo)* apartments. Vignamaggio stands out from them all: one of those rare places that made us think twice about advertising it. The villa's first owners were the Gherardini family, of which Mona Lisa, born here in 1479, was a member. This could even have been where she and Leonardo met. More recently, it was the setting for Kenneth Branagh's film of Shakespeare's *Much Ado About Nothing.*

Villa di Vignamaggio is a warm Tuscan pink. A small formal garden in front gives way to acres of vines. The pool, a short distance from the house, is among fields and trees. The interior is a perfect combination of simplicity and good taste, with the emphasis on natural materials. Beds, chairs and sofas are comfortable and attractive. Old wardrobes cleverly hide small kitchen units. The two public rooms are equally pleasing, and breakfast there or on the terrace is thoughtfully planned, with bread from the local bakery and home-made jam. The staff were charming and helpful when we visited 'Service' is kept to a minimum ("This is *not* a hotel").

Nearby Greve (5 km); Florence (19 km); Siena (38 km).

Greve in Chianti, 50022
Florence
Tel (055) 8544840
Fax (055) 8544468
Location on its own estate,
5 km SE of Greve on the road
to Lamole from the SS222
Meals breakfast; dinner on
two evenings a week
Prices LL-LLLL
Rooms 11 double-bedded
mini-apartments, two in separate cottages, each with bath,

kitchen and heating
Facilities sitting-room, bar,
terrace, garden, swimming-
pool, tennis court, children's
playground, walks
Credit cards AE, EC, MC, V
Children welcome
Disabled one apartment
Pets welcome
Closed never
Languages English, German,
French
Proprietor Gianni Nunziante

Firenze

Il Burchio

A small plaque bearing the words 'Club Ippico' (Riding Club) is the only outward sign that Il Burchio, reached by a winding dir track, is not a private house. Alda Crespi runs her family home as a club, not a hotel. You will especially like it if you are keen on riding or Italian cookery, and if you are happy socializing with othe guests in a friendly house-party environment.

The buildings were restored in 1995 and 1996, and the result is a simple but comfortable country house: whitewashed walls, terracot ta floors, rustic wooden furniture, wrought-iron bedsteads, and plenty of pretty floral fabrics.

Traditional Tuscan meals are eaten communally at one enor mous table and guests are encouraged to chat with one another. The presence of several guitars and a piano often bring on bouts o singing and music-making after dinner.

The ambience is genuinely friendly and informal, and comfort able for any age group. A stable of 17 horses provides trekking and riding lessons, while cookery courses with a local expert take place in the kitchen.

Nearby Florence (25 km). S. Giovanni Valdarno.

Via Poggio al Burchio, 4,
Incisa Valdarno, 50064
Firenze
Tel (055) 8330124
Fax (055) 8330234
Location off a tiny side road,
2 km N of Incisa Valdarno, in
own grounds with ample
parking
Meals breakfast, lunch on
request, dinner
Prices L; suites LL
Rooms 1 single, 8 double,
3 suites; all with shower, TV

on request, heating
Facilities sitting-room,
restaurant, bar, courtyard
terrace, garden, small pool,
riding, cookery courses
Credit cards EC, MC, V
Children welcome
Disabled not suitable
Pets small dogs and cats
welcome (room with roof
access)
Closed 5 Nov to 15 Mar
Languages some English
Proprietor Alda Crespi

Firenze

Country guest-house, Mercatale Val di Pesa

Salvadonica

Two enterprising sisters have turned their family's 14thC farm properties into a thriving guest-house and apartment complex, in rolling countryside, south of Florence, a conversion carried out with style and panache, exploiting the buildings' character and position to the maximum. The central house is a warm pink and is surrounded by stone farmhouses with their details picked out in brick. In the paved courtyard stands a single umbrella pine. The enthusiasm of Francesca and Beatrice and their friendly welcome makes for a vivacious, friendly atmosphere.

Elegance and comfort characterize the rooms and apartments, with individual variations on the classic rustic ingredients of beamed ceilings, simple white plaster walls and warm, terracotta-tiled floors. A particularly impressive apartment with refined brick vaulting and columns looks more like the crypt of a Renaissance church than a converted cow byre. With a swimming-pool, tennis-court and riding (nearby) as well as easy access to Tuscany's most important art cities, your stay at Salvadonica will seem all too short. A recent visitor was thoroughly enchanted.
Nearby Florence (18 km); Siena (40 km).

Via Grevigiana 82, 50024
Mercatale Val di Pesa
(Firenze)
Tel (055) 8218039
Fax (055) 8218043
Location 18 km S of Florence,
leaving Siena highway (SS2) at
San Casciano Val di Pesa; own
grounds, ample parking
Meals breakfast, snacks
Prices LL-LLL
Rooms 5 double, all with bath
or shower, phone; 10
apartments for two to four
persons, rentable daily
according to availability
Facilities breakfast-room,
garden, swimming-pool,
billiards, tennis
Smoking not in breakfast-room
Credit cards AE, DC, EC, MC,
V **Children** welcome
Disabled two adapted rooms
Pets not accepted **Closed** Nov
to Feb
Languages English, German
Proprietors Beatrice and
Francesca Baccetti

Firenze

Country villa, Montefiridolfi

Il Borghetto

Discretion, taste and refinement are the key characteristics of this family guest-house, only recently opened but already appreciated by a discerning (and returning) clientèle that enjoys civilized living in a peaceful, bucolic setting.

A manicured gravel drive, leads past the lawn, with its rose beds and cypress trees, to the main buildings, which include the remains of two 15thC military towers. From a covered terrace, where breakfast is accompanied by views of miles of open countryside, a broad-arched entrance leads to the open-plan ground floor of the main villa. Within, the usual starkness of the Tuscan style has been softened by the use of muted tones in the wall colours and fabrics. Comfortable furniture abounds without cluttering the spacious, airy quality of the public areas. Upstairs, in the bedrooms (some of which are not particularly large), floral wallpaper and subdued lighting create a balmy, relaxed atmosphere. No intrusive phone calls or blaring televisions; a mini-bar would be considered vulgar.

Even the refined like a swim; but for those who consider swimming-pools raucous, there is a soothing water garden.

Nearby Florence (18 km); Siena (45 km); San Gimignano (40 km).

Via Collina S Angelo 23, Montefiridolfi, S. Casciano Val di Pesa, 50020 Firenze
Tel (055) 8244442
Fax (055) 8244247
Location hillside villa in its own grounds; ample car parking
Meals breakfast; lunch and dinner if sufficient numbers request
Prices LLL; 2-day min. stay
Rooms 6 doubles, 2 suites all with shower

Facilities sitting-room, dining-room, terrace, gardens, swimming-pool, cookery courses
Smoking allowed
Credit cards EC, MC, V
Children not suitable for very young children
Disabled one suitable room with bathroom **Pets** not accepted **Closed** Nov to Mar
Languages English, French, German
Manager Antonio Cavallini

Firenze

Villa Le Barone

One of the great delights of aristocrats finding their villas too large and expensive to run is that, when they retire to the tastefully converted chicken-house, they leave behind them family collections of antiques, paintings and *objets d'art*, painstakingly put together over the centuries, which no interior decorator could hope to imitate. Such is the case with Le Barone, a small gem of a villa, which still retains the atmosphere of a private house rather than a hotel.

An air of unforced refinement and aristocratic ease in a setting of withdrawn tranquillity will immediately strike any visitor. The public rooms are small in scale and slightly cluttered; in the sitting-room, with its blue and yellow sofas, dominated at one end by a carved-stone fireplace, there is a collection of family paintings and of books which you are welcome to read. Just outside, is a long gravel terrace, for breakfast in fine weather or drinks in the evening. The bar, where you help yourself and write it down in a book, has seats made from wine-barrels and a cradle full of flowers. Bedrooms, particularly those in the main villa (reached by a spiral staircase), are tastefully furnished.

Nearby Greve (6 km); Florence (29 km); Siena (33 km).

Via San Leolino 19, Panzano
in Chianti,, 50020 Firenze
Tel (055) 852621
Fax (055) 852277
Location 6 km S of Greve in
Chianti in its own grounds;
ample car parking
Meals breakfast, lunch,
dinner, snacks
Prices LLL (DB&B) (min 3
nights)
Rooms 25 double, all with
bath or shower, phone; 5 with

air-conditioning
Facilities sitting-rooms,
breakfast-room, restaurant,
bar, swimming-pool, tennis
Smoking permitted
Credit cards AE, MC, V
Children welcome
Disabled not suitable
Pets dogs not allowed
Closed Nov to Mar
Languages English
Proprietor Duchessa Franca
di Grazzano Visconti

Firenze

Country villa, Panzano in Chianti

Villa Sangiovese

The Bleulers once managed the Tenuta di Ricavo at Castellin (page 85). It's now more than ten years since they started this new venture in Panzano, a few miles to the north. Readers' reports ar consistently appreciative.

The main villa is a neat stone-and-stucco house fronting direct on to a back-street; potted plants and a brass plate besid the doorway are the only signs of a hotel. Attached to this hous is an old rambling stone building beside a flowery, gravelle courtyard-terrace offering splendid views. The landscaped garde below includes a fair-sized pool. Inside, all is mellow, welcomin and stylish, with carefully chosen antique furnishings against plain pale walls. Bedrooms, some with wood-beamed ceilings are spacious, comfortably, and tastefully restrained in decoration. Th dining-room is equally simple and stylish, with subdued wall ligh ing and bentwood chairs on a tiled floor.

A limited but interestng *à la carte* menu is offered, which change each night – service on the terrace in summer. A recent reporte praised the food and the wine.

Nearby Greve (5 km); Siena (30 km); Florence (30 km).

Piazza Bucciarelli 5, 50020 Panzano in Chianti, Firenze
Tel (055) 852461
Fax (055) 852463
Location on edge of town, 5 km S of Greve; with large garden and ample car parking
Meals breakfast, lunch, dinner
Prices rooms LLL; suites LLLLL; meals from LL
Rooms 15 double, 1 single, 3 suites, all with bath or shower; all rooms have phone
Facilities dining-room, 2 sitting-rooms, library, bar, terrace, swimming-pool
Credit cards MC, V
Children accepted
Disabled no special facilities
Pets not accepted
Closed Jan, Feb; restaurant only, Wed
Manager Ulderico and Anna Maria Bleuler

Hilltop villa, Reggello

Villa Rigacci

This creeper-covered 15thC farmhouse stands in a beautiful secluded spot – a hill-top surrounded by olive groves, pines, chestnut
trees and meadows – yet only a few kilometres from the Florence-
Rome *autostrada* and a short drive from Florence and Arezzo.

The house achieves a cosy and relaxed atmosphere in spite of its
four-star facilities. It is furnished as a cherished family home, much
of it reflecting Signor Pierazzi's Camargue background, including
some lovely antiques from the region and prints of Camargue horses. Bedrooms – the best are gloriously spacious and full of gleaming antiques – overlook the gardens and tranquil swimming-pool.

The sitting-room has an open fire in chilly weather; the breakfast-room is a converted stable with the hay racks still on the walls.
The elegantly rustic dining-room has a sophisticated Mediter-
ranean menu. Guests are well cared for – if you are peckish, for
example, you can order snacks or light meals at any time of the
day. In summer, fish and meat are cooked *al fresco* on the large outdoor barbecue. Next to the house is a tiny family chapel where
Mass is still occasionally said.
Nearby Florence (35 km); Arezzo (45 km).

Vággio 76, Regello 50066,
Florence
Tel (055) 865 6718
Fax (055) 865 6537
Location 300 m N of Vággio,
30 km SE of Florence; exit
Incisa from A1; with car
parking and shady, tree-filled
gardens
Meals breakfast, lunch,
dinner
Prices LL-LLL
Rooms 3 single, 15 double,
4 suites; all with bath and

shower, TV, minibar, air-
conditioning, heating, phone
Facilities sitting-room,
restaurant, bar, terrace,
garden, pool
Credit cards AE, DC, EC, MC,
V
Children welcome
Disabled no special facilities
Pets accepted
Closed never
Languages English, German,
French, Spanish, Arabic
Proprietor Federico Pierazzi

Firenze

Town villa, Sesto Fiorentino

Villa Villoresi

The aristocratic Villa Villoresi looks rather out of place in what is now an industrial suburb of Florence, but once in the house and gardens you suddenly feel a million miles away from modern bustling Florence. Contessa Cristina Villoresi is a warm hostess who has captured the hearts of many transatlantic and other guests. It is thanks to her that the villa still has the feel of a private home – all rather grand, if a little faded and standing still in time.

As you make your way through the building, each room seems to have some curiosity or feature of the past. The entrance hall is a superb gallery of massive chandeliers, frescoed walls, antiques and lofty potted plants. Then there is the first-floor loggia, the longest in Tuscany, on to which five of the finest bedrooms open. Another on the ground floor, has crystal chandeliers, floor-to-ceiling frescoes, and a canopied bed. Other bedrooms, however, are very different: small and plain with simple painted furniture, and looking on to an inner courtyard.

In the two dining-rooms Tuscan specialities are served. Contessa Villoresi runs residential courses on the Italian Renaissance.
Nearby Florence (8 km).

Via Campi 2, Colonnata di
Sesto Fiorentino, 50019
Firenze
Tel (055) 443212
Fax (055) 442063
E-mail cvillor.tin.it
Location 9 km NW of
Florence; adequate parking
Meals breakfast, lunch,
dinner
Prices rooms LL-LLLL;
DB&B LLL with breakfast;
meals LL; 10% reductions
mid-Jul to Sept, Nov to Easter
and for children
Rooms 23 double, 5 single;
all with bath, shower, TV on
request, heating, phone
Facilities sitting-rooms, res-
taurant, bar, terraces, garden,
pool, walks **Credit cards** AE,
DC, MC, V **Children** welcome
Disabled ground floor rooms
Pets not in public rooms
Closed never **Languages**
English, German, French
Proprietor Contessa Cristina
Villoresi

Firenze

Villa hotel, Trespiano

Villa Le Rondini

The swallows that give the hotel its name can be seen in the evening, skimming over one of the most pleasant swimming-pools in the Florence area, set in shady olive groves and with a view over the city second to none. One of the most attractive features of Villa Le Rondini is its enviable location: only seven kilometres from Florence's crowded centre (reachable by bus) yet in the middle of acres of parkland on top of Monte Rinaldi, north of the city. The grounds are a delight to wander through.

The long, ochre-coloured, 16thC villa is surrounded by lawns and terraces, and contains the principal public rooms and the main bedrooms (the remainder are in two other more modern buildings nearby). The furnishings are a not completely successful eclectic mixture of rustic antiques and outdated hotel furniture. The sitting-room is full of comfortable couches and chairs, dominated at one end by an immense, carved stone fireplace.

Bedrooms vary in size and furnishings, some with wrought-iron beds and antiques, others more modern in style; the suites have the best views. All have decent bathrooms.

Nearby Florence (7 km); Mugello valley.

Via Bolognese Vecchia 224, Trespiano, 50139 Firenze
Tel (055) 400081
Fax (055) 268212
Location 7 km north of Florence on the old road to Bologna, in own grounds; plenty of parking
Meals breakfast, lunch, dinner
Prices LL-LLL
Rooms 43 double, all with bath or shower, phone, TV, minibar, air-conditioning

Facilities sitting-rooms, restaurant, conference room, park, swimming-pool with bar, tennis, riding, heliport
Smoking allowed
Credit cards AE, DC, EC, MC, V
Children welcome
Disabled some suitable rooms
Pets please check first
Closed never
Languages English, French, German
Manager Francesca Reali

Firenze

Country hotel, Vicchio

Villa Campestri

Mugello is the name of the little-visited area north-east of Florence characterized by dramatic mountain landscapes bordering wide river valleys. Wilder than Chianti, it is increasingly frequented by Florentines in search of unspoilt countryside without the billboards that are becoming eyesores in the more popular parts of Tuscany. Unfortunately, you will not find too many decent hotels either, and Villa Campestri is by far the most stylish in the area.

The Renaissance villa, a square, imposing building in off-white stucco, stands on top of a hill in open countryside. Before being turned into a hotel it was owned by the same family for over six hundred years. Much of its former grandeur remains: on the ground floor, stately public rooms paved in stone or dark terracotta are hung with faded tapestries and oil paintings. One of them has fine stained windows executed by Chini in Liberty style. The restaurant is one of the best in the area. It is also a popular place for wedding parties, which can be a nuisance at weekends.)
Bedrooms are equally grand in the villa, though a few more homely ones have been added in the next-door farmhouse.
Nearby Florence (35 km).

Via di Campestri 19/22,
Vicchio di Mugello, 50039
Firenze
Tel (055) 8490107
Fax (055) 8490108
Location 3 km S of Vicchio,
in own grounds; ample car
parking
Meals breakfast, dinner,
snacks
Prices LL-LLL
Rooms 14 double, 6 suites, 1
single, all with bath or shower, phone, satellite TV, mini-bar
Facilities sitting-rooms,
restaurant, bar, swimming-pool, horse-riding; golf
nearby
Smoking allowed
Credit cards EC, MC, V
Children welcome
Disabled 4 adapted rooms
Pets small dogs, only on
request
Closed Jan to Mar
Languages English
Proprietor Paolo Pasquali

Lucca

Country villa, Lucca

Villa la Principessa Elisa

French official of the Napoleonic times who accompanied the Emperor's sister, Elisa Baciocchi, to Lucca acquired this 18thC villa for his own residence. Perhaps that accounts for the discernibly French style of the house that makes it unique among Tuscan hotels. A square building, three storeys high, painted in an arresting blue with windows and cornices picked out in gleaming white, the villa stands just off the busy old Pisa-Lucca road.

The restorers have fortunately avoided the oppressive Empire style (which, in any case, the small rooms would not have borne) and aimed throughout at lightness and delicacy. The entrance is a symphony in wood, with geometrically patterned parquet flooring and panelled walls, and the illusion of space created with large mirrors. To the right is a small sitting-room, furnished with fine antiques and Knole sofas. A round 19thC conservatory is now the restaurant. Each suite has been individually decorated using striped, floral and small-check patterns and yet more antiques – no expense has been spared. Sister hotel of the Principessa across the road, the Elisa is a notable step up in taste and refinement.

Nearby Lucca (3 km); Pisa (15 km).

Via Nuova per Pisa (SS 12
bis), Massa Pisana, 55050
Lucca
Tel (0583) 379737
Fax (0583) 379019
Location 3 km S of Lucca on
the old road to Pisa, in its
own grounds; car parking
Meals breakfast, lunch,
dinner
Prices LLL-LLLL
Rooms 1 double, 1 single,
3 suites, all with bath or
shower, phone, TV, air-
conditioning
Facilities sitting-rooms,
garden, swimming-pool
Smoking allowed
Credit cards AE, DC, EC, MC,
V **Children** welcome but 3rd
beds are not possible
Disabled some ground floor
rooms but no special
bathrooms **Pets** small dogs
(surcharge) **Closed** early Jan
to early Feb **Languages**
English, German **Proprietor**
Giancarlo Mugnani

Lucca

Country villa, Santa Maria del Giudice

Villa Rinascimento

Almost exactly half-way between Pisa and Lucca, this hillside vil
presents, at first sight, something of an architectural conundrum
On the right-hand side is a rosy coloured, rustic Renaissance vill
three storeys high, constructed with a mixture of brick and ston
Its main feature is a lovely corner loggia, enclosed by four bri
arches supported by Doric columns in stone. On the left, it
joined by a much simpler farmhouse structure. The two are unite
by a long, paved terrace with lemon trees in large terracotta po
One can breakfast here or take an *aperitivo* in the evening.

Inside, a more uniform rustic style prevails. The public roor
are all in a row, facing the terrace, and distinguished by havir
either exposed-beam or brick-vaulted ceilings, all immaculate
restored and including interesting features such as the remnants
an old stone olive-press. Great effort has been put into the be
room furnishings. Some of the bathrooms are small, but adequat

Up the hill from the villa is the annex, with some more mode
rooms and studios, and a pool designed to exploit to the full
hillside position.

Nearby Lucca (9 km); Pisa (11 km).

Loc. Santa Maria del Giudice, 55058 Lucca **Tel** (0583) 378292 **Fax** (0583) 370238 **Location** 9 km SW of Lucca in its own grounds; ample car parking **Meals** breakfast, dinner **Prices** L-LL **Rooms** 17 double, all with bath or shower, phone; some with TV; 4 simpler rooms and 6 studios (one-week rents from Saturdays) in annexe	**Facilities** sitting-rooms, bar, restaurant, swimming-pool **Smoking** allowed **Credit cards** EC, MC, V **Children** welcome **Disabled** one room with bathroom **Pets** please check first **Closed** Nov to Mar; restaurant only, Wed **Languages** English, German, French, Dutch **Proprietor** Carla Zaffora

Pisa

Farmhouse, Montecatini Val di Cecina

Il Frassinello

The difficult unsurfaced road that brings you from Montecatini to Il Frassinello seems to last for ever and is certainly not for the weak-spirited. But it is also a guarantee of seclusion. You arrive at your destination to be greeted by the redoubtable Signora Schlubach, who decided to retire here and "not see too much action".

If ever a place has received the imprint of its owner, this is it. The spacious, pleasantly proportioned interiors are filled with the results of a lifetime's collecting on various continents: zebra rugs on the floors, the mounted heads of at least four different types of antelope, a bronze angel hovering over the kitchen door.

There are three rooms in the main villa, and four large self-contained apartments with new bathrooms in a separate building, each with a little kitchen and their own entrance and private terrace, where the minimum stay is three nights.

Guests are not expected to do very much: just relax, take a stroll down to the deer farm, or read a book. Breakfast is taken either in the homely kitchen, or outside under the wisteria-covered pergola.
Nearby Volterra (23 km).

Montecatini Val di Cecina,
56040 Pisa
Tel (0588) 30080
Fax (0588) 30080
Location 5 km from
Montecatini Val di Cecina in
middle of countryside
Meals breakfast; dinner on
request (sometimes)
Prices rooms L; apartment
LLLL per week; discounts for
longer stays
Rooms 4 double all with bath

or shower; 4 apartments
Facilities sitting-room,
garden
Smoking allowed
Credit cards not accepted
Children welcome
Disabled not suitable
Pets small dogs
Closed Oct to Easter
Languages English, French,
German, Spanish
Proprietor Elga Schlubach

Pistoia

Country Villa, Massa e Cozzile

Villa Pasquini

Stay at Villa Pasquini and you step back into the 19thC. Little ha▊
changed here, either in furnishings, or decoration, since then
Until five years ago, it was the autumn retreat of an aristocrati▊
Roman family, the Pasquinis; then it was bought, fully furnished, b▊
the present incumbents, who have lovingly preserved it, combinin▊
a family home with a most unusual hotel. Though it is somethin▊
of a museum piece, the atmosphere is not stuffy. The family'▊
enthusiasm is infectious, and the welcome warm.

The bedrooms are, of course, all different, some quite grand▊
(but not intimidating) with canopied beds. Bathrooms are old-fash▊
ioned, but well equipped. Many boast wonderful *trompe l`oeil* fres▊
coes – lie in your tub contemplating a lakeland scene with swan▊
and distant mountains.

In the attractive dining-room – originally the entrance hall – th▊
emphasis is on traditional recipes. Our reporter chose the fixed▊
price menu, was served five delicious courses and thought the pric▊
very reasonable.

Outside, the gardens and terraces are lush with flowers.

Nearby Montecatini Terme (8 km); Lucca (40 km); Pisa (60 km);

Via Vacchereccia 56, Margine
Coperta, Massa e Cozzile,
51010 Pistoia
Tel (0572) 72205
Fax (0572) 910888
Location off minor road 6 km
N of Montecatini Terme
in own grounds; ample
car parking
Meals breakfast, dinner
Prices doubles L
Rooms 12 double, all with
bath and shower, central
heating
Facilities 2 sitting-rooms,
dining-room, terraces,
garden, walks
Credit cards AE, EC, MC, V
Children welcome
Disabled some suitable rooms
Pets not accepted
Closed 30 Nov to 15 Mar
Languages English, German,
French
Proprietors Innocenti family

Pistoia

Farmhouse bed-and-breakfast, Montevettolini

Villa Lucia

ucia Vallera also calls her delightful hillside farmhouse the 'B & B
Tuscany' and runs her establishment along English bed-and-
eakfast lines – guests and family mingle informally, eating togeth-
in the traditional Tuscan kitchen or at the huge wooden table in
e dining-room if numbers require.

A strong Californian influence can be felt in the cooking and in
e laid-back, elegant style of the place. (Lucia is an American of
lian extraction who has recently returned to Italy after living in
e States.) There are plenty of up-to-date touches: CD player,
tellite TV, computer. The clientèle, too, is mainly American –
yers, doctors and so on – often on return visits.

The dining-room has various dressers crammed with colourful
ina and glass; there is a double sitting-room with comfortable
fas and armchairs in traditional fabrics, plus shelves of books.
drooms are attractive, with working fireplaces, patchwork bed-
reads, terracotta floors and antique furniture. Bathrooms are
cked in blue and white tiles, and spotless. The house has a lovely
rden, and looks up to the old town of Montevettolini.

earby Montecatini Terme, Lucca, Vinci.

ia dei Bronzoli 144,
Iontevettolini, 51010 Pistoia
el (0572) 617790
ax (0572) 628817
.ocation on hillside outside
Iontevettolini, in own
rounds, with ample car
arking
Meals breakfast; dinner on
equest
rices LL-LLL
Rooms 5 double, 2
apartments for 2; all with
ath and shower, either

adjoining or across the hall,
all with heating
Facilities sitting-room,
conference room, terraces,
garden, small pool
Credit cards none
Children welcome
Disabled no special facilities
Pets not accepted
Closed Nov to Apr
Languages English, French,
Spanish, German
Proprietor Lucia Vallera

Pistoia

Agriturismo apartments, Pescia

Marzalla

A family-run Agriturismo set in the Pistoiese hills near the old to
of Pescia: not an idyllic Chianti setting, but pleasant enough, a
with the benefit of fewer tourists than elsewhere.

Candida Cecchi is a lively and helpful young hostess. She a
her family live in a vast, crumbling 16thC villa and have conver
nearby farm buildings into five apartments. They are simply
attractively decorated in rustic style, three with open fires, all w
white walls, wooden beams, antique furniture. Colourful touch
add interest: Indian bedspreads, brightly coloured duvets and bl
kets. Four of the apartments are large and well-equipped, with t
or three double rooms and separate living areas; one is a cute s
dio apartment. All have private gardens with tables and chairs.

Unusually for an Agriturismo, a separate restaurant provides
ditional Tuscan meals: Candida's mother-in-law presides. This is
unpretentious place for a stay off the beaten track, but well plac
for sightseeing; it's in good walking country, too. The modern su
urbs of Pescia and its expanse of greenhouses somewhat mar t
view, but overall Marzalla offers value for money.

Nearby Lucca (18 km); Montecatini Terme (8 km); Pistoiese hil

Via Collecchio 1, Pescia,
51017 Pistoia
Tel (0572) 490751
Fax (0572) 478332
Location on the N outskirts
of Pescia, in own grounds,
with car parking
Meals breakfast, dinner
Prices L; dinner L30,000
Rooms 5 apartments,
available per week (3 nights
min. in off season); 3 double
rooms available for min. 2-
night stays; all rooms have

bath, shower, phone, heating
TV in apartments only
Facilities restaurant,
conference room, terraces,
garden, swimming-pool
Credit cards not accepted
Children welcome
Disabled one apartment
adapted for wheelchairs
Pets in apartments, but not
in rooms **Closed** never
Languages English, French
Proprietor Candida Cecchi
de Rossi

Pistoia

Country Villa, Pistoia

Villa Vannini

ere is a real gem, well off the beaten track, and a complete con-
ast to the usual Tuscan villa. It has an Alpine feel: fir trees all
ound; low ceilings; green shutters; a little Swiss-style clock tower –
d miles of marked footpaths all around, eventually leading up to
e ski resort of Abetone. It is a haven for serious walkers (Signora
annini organizes guided walking tours in the surrounding
mote, wooded hills).

The atmosphere at Villa Vannini is that of a private country
ouse: there are no hotel signs. You will be greeted by an over-
thusiastic dog. An inviting smell of wood smoke pervades. The
od served in the charming dining-room or on the terrace under
ge white umbrellas is carefully prepared and elegantly present-
. Breakfasts are 'excellent' too, according to a recent reporter.
edrooms are well above the standard for the price, beautifully and
dividually furnished, with polished parquet floors, oriental rugs,
ass or wood bedsteads and lovely antique furniture and mirrors.

Signora Vannini, with her sense of humour and fund of stories,
the making of this place, and her staff are evidently devoted.

earby Pistoia, Florence (25 km); Lucca (25 km); Pistoiese hills.

Villa di Piteccio, 51030 Pistoia
Tel (0573) 42031
Fax (0573) 26331
Location 6 km N of Pistoia on
hillside, in private garden,
with car parking
Meals breakfast, lunch,
dinner
Prices doubles LLL (reductions for minimum of 3 days'
stay); dinner L30,000 without
wine
Rooms 8 double with bath

and central heating
Facilities 2 sitting-rooms,
games room, dining-room,
terrace
Credit cards EC, MC, V
Children not suitable
Disabled no special facilities
Pets not accepted
Closed never
Languages English, German,
French
Proprietor Maria-Rosa
Vannini

Prato

Country guest-house, Bacchereto

Fattoria di Bacchereto

One of the most attractive aspects of Fattoria di Bacchereto is i
location high in the steep foothills of the Appenines, part of th
famous Carmignano wine-growing district (which produces Italy
oldest recognized wine). Entirely isolated, with panoramic view
this little-frequented part of Tuscany is perfect for those who like
combine some city tourism (Florence, Pistoia, Lucca and Pisa a
all within driving distance) with country walks and rural peace.

But do not expect luxury: the Fattoria is a working farm and th
accommodation is relatively simple. The bedrooms and apartmen
are spread across the main villa, a rambling 18thC building wit
terraces and an arched loggia, and simpler farmhouses nearb
The rooms are furnished with time-worn rustic antiques, some
need of restoration, in a setting of terracotta floors and expose
beam ceilings. The bathrooms are basic but functional.

Outside the villa are pergolas and an ornamental garden with
pond and a fountain, and slightly down the hillside is a small swim
ming-pool. Breakfast is eaten at a long table near the kitchen; fo
other meals there is the excellent family restaurant nearby.

Nearby Florence (25 km); Pistoia (18 km).

Loc. Bacchereto, Via
Fontemorana 179, 50042
Prato
Tel (055) 8717191
Fax (055) 8717191
Location 20 km W of
Florence, near Carmignano,
in own grounds; car parking
Meals breakfast
Prices L
Rooms 7 double, some with
private bathrooms;
3 apartments for 4 to 6
persons

Facilities breakfast-room,
sitting-room, gardens,
swimming-pool; family
restaurant nearby
Smoking allowed
Credit cards not accepted
Children welcome
Disabled not suitable
Pets not accepted
Closed never
Languages English, French,
Spanish
Proprietor Carlo Bencini Tesi

Prato

Villa Rucellai

Industrial Prato creeps almost to the door of this mellow old villa, and a railway line skirts the property, but this should not deter you from staying in this special place. The views from the loggia and lovely terrace – filled with lemon trees – are unsightly, but are more than compensated for by the cultured atmosphere of the house, the warm welcome and the modest prices. Behind the estate rise the beautiful Pratese hills, which can be explored on foot from the house.

The origins of the Villa Rucellai date back to a medieval watch-tower, and it has been in the venerable Rucellai family since 1740. Guests have the run of the main part of the house, with its baronial hall and comfortable, lived-in sitting-room, filled with pictures and books. Breakfast is self-service and eaten around a communal table in the homely dining-room. Bedrooms are simply furnished and full of character, reflecting what a recent visitor confirmed is the main and rare attribute of the place – that of a simple but well-run hotel which gives no hint of being anything other than a cultivated family house.

Nearby Prato; Florence (20 km).

Via di Canneto 16, Prato, 50047 Firenze
Tel (0574) 460392
Location in narrow street in Bisenzio river valley, 4 km NE of Prato, (keep parallel with river and train tracks on your left); car parking and grounds
Meals breakfast
Prices rooms LL
Rooms 12 double, one family room; 10 rooms have bath or shower; all have central heating; some have phone
Facilities dining-room, sitting-room, TV room, gymnasium, terrace, swimming-pool
Credit cards not accepted
Children welcome; cots and high chairs by arrangement
Disabled not suitable
Pets not usually accepted
Closed never **Languages** English **Proprietors** Rucellai Piqué family

Siena

Country hotel, Castellina in Chianti

Belvedere di San Leonino

Tourism has been booming in Chianti over the past few years, especially in the commune of Castellina. It is easy to see why: rolling countryside liberally sprinkled with villas, the great art cities within driving distance and a surplus of farmhouses left by people migrating to the cities.

San Leonino is a typical case: a squat, square 15thC house with its barn and stables, built from the light-coloured local stone. The farmyard has been turned into a garden. A tree-shaded terrace has been created at the back, right at the edge of the vineyards, and tucked away out of sight is the swimming-pool. The restoration of the interiors has been meticulously done so that it is difficult to believe that the house is more than five hundred years old.

Sitting areas have been created out of the stables: wide, open rooms spanned by crescent-shaped brick arches. If we have one complaint, it is that the furnishing here would be more suitable for an airport lounge than a Tuscan farmhouse: the long, anonymous modern couches clash badly with the rustic ambience. Bedrooms are of a much higher standard. Prices are good value for this area.

Nearby Siena (15 km); San Gimignano (30 km); Florence (50 km).

Loc. S. Leonino, Castellina in
Chianti 53011 Siena
Tel (0577) 740887
Fax (0577) 740924
Location 15 km N of Siena, in
its own grounds; car parking
Meals breakfast, dinner,
lunch on request
Prices LL
Rooms 28 double, all with
bath or shower, phone
Facilities sitting-room,
restaurant, bar, terrace,
gardens, swimming-pool
Smoking permitted
Credit cards AE, EC, MC, V
Children welcome
Disabled not suitable
Pets not accepted
Closed mid-Nov to mid-Mar
Languages English, French,
German
Proprietor Marco Orlandi

Country hotel, Castellina in Chianti

Il Colombaio

new addition to the typically Tuscan farmhouse hotels that clus-
r around Castellina in Chianti, Il Colombaio is a successful exam-
e of a proven formula, and at a very reasonable price. As you
me from Greve in Chianti on the busy Chiantigiana road (SS
2), you will notice on the right this farmhouse surrounded by
wns, shrubs and trees. Stone-built and capped with the tiled roofs
odd angles to one another so characteristic of Tuscany, the
use has a pleasing aspect. It is, however, close to the road.

The restoration has been carried out with attention to detail,
sing country furniture to complement the rustic style of the build-
g. The sitting-room, which used to be the farm kitchen, is spa-
ous and light with beamed ceilings, a traditional open fireplace
d, in the corner, the old stone sink now filled with house-plants.
reakfast is served in a small stone-vaulted room on the terrace.

Fifteen of the bedrooms are in the main house (the other six are
an annex across the road) and have been furnished with
rought-iron beds and old-fashioned dressing tables; all have mod-
n bathrooms.

earby Siena (20 km); Florence (40 km); San Gimignano (30 km).

Via Chiantigiana 29,
Castellina in Chianti 53011
Siena
Tel (0577) 740444
Fax (0577) 740444
Location just N of Castellina,
in own grounds; car parking
Meals breakfast
Prices LL
Rooms 21 double, all with
bath or shower
Facilities sitting-room,
breakfast-room, garden,

swimming-pool
Smoking allowed
Credit cards AE, DC, EC, MC,
V
Children welcome
Disabled some facilities
Pets please check first
Closed never
Languages English, French,
German
Manager Roberta Baldini

Siena

Town hotel, Castellina in Chianti

Palazzo Squarcialupi

Palazzo Squarcialupi is set right in the heart of the Medieval villag
of Castellina in Chianti, and when our reporter first visited, s
was struck by the friendly, peaceful atmosphere and the love
rooms.

It is a 14thC stone building with arched doors and window
which was formerly an imposing farm residence. It has bee
renovated in a simple, stylish way, while retaining its tradition
farm character. There are seventeen large bedrooms and suit
with plain white walls, beamed ceilings and dark wooden furnitur
downstairs is a rustic sitting-room in muted tones of white, crea
and terracotta, and another elegant room with frescoes.

Palazzo Squarcialupi is bound to delight those with an intere
in sampling the local wine. Chianti Classico continues to l
produced in the Fattoria, and barrels of 'La Castellina', the hou
wine, line the stone-vaulted cellar. Guests can taste the vintages
the bar or in the wine-tasting room, or on the terrace while adm
ing magnificent views of the Chianti countryside. New to the guid
reports welcome.

Nearby Siena (18 km); Florence (40 km); San Gimignano (30 km

Via Ferruccio, 26 Castellina
in Chianti 53011 Siena
Tel (0577) 741186
Fax (0577) 740386
Location in town centre,
overlooking valley
Meals buffet breakfast; light
meals in the bar
Prices LL-LLL
Rooms 9 double; 8 suites; all
with bath or shower; all
rooms have phone, TV, minibar, central heating, air-
conditioning
Facilities breakfast-room, 2
sitting-rooms, bar, terrace,
garden, pool, wine cellar
Smoking permitte
Credit cards MC, V
Children welcome; cradle
and cots free **Disabled** 2
suitable rooms **Pets** small pets
accepted **Closed** mid-Jan to
mid-Mar **Languages** English,
French, German, Spanish
Proprietors Targioni family

Siena

Country hotel, Castellina in Chianti

Le Piazze

A welcome addition to the booming hotel scene in the area around Castellina in Chianti which, we feel, has the edge on many of its competitors. Although only 6 km from the bustling town, the hotel is in completely secluded countryside reached by a long unsurfaced road which seems to go on forever the first time around.

The hotel is, needless to say, a converted 17thC farmhouse, but in this case the owners have deployed more imagination and a greater sense of elegance than usual. The buffet breakfast, for instance, is served on tiled sideboards in a room adjacent to the kitchen and separated from it by a glass partition. Or you can remove yourself to any of the numerous terraces that surround the house for uninterrupted views of classical Chianti countryside.

Rustic antiques have, of course, been used in the furnishing with the usual terracotta/exposed beam/white plaster, but with the interesting idea of adding pieces from Indonesia. Bedrooms are individually furnished with lavish use of striped fabrics (avoid those in the roof space – they can become unbearably hot); bathrooms are large, with Jacuzzis or walk-in showers big enough for a party.
Nearby Siena (27 km); Florence (50 km).

Loc. Le Piazze, Castellina in Chianti, 53011 Siena
Tel (0577) 743190
Fax (0577) 743191
Location 6 km W of Castellina in its own grounds; ample car parking
Meals breakfast, lunch and dinner on request
Prices LL-LLL; special inclusive weekend offers in winter
Rooms 15 double, all with bath or shower, phone

Facilities sitting-room, breakfast-room, bar, terrace, gardens, swimming-pool
Smoking permitted
Credit cards AE, DC, EC, MC, V
Children over-12s welcome
Disabled one adapted room
Pets non-barking dogs
Closed never
Languages English, French, German
Proprietor Maureen Skelly Bonini

Siena

Country hotel, Castellina in Chianti

Salivolpi

We remain pleasantly surprised by the excellent value offered by the Salivolpi in this popular part of Chianti. Prices for a double have not increased significantly, a sure sign of high advance bookings and a satisfied clientèle that returns year after year. Not that this country guest-house in any way resembles a cheap alternative. Of the many converted farmhouses in the area, Salivolpi has the edge not just in terms of price but also because of its pleasant grounds and its swimming-pool.

The buildings consist of the low stone farmhouses typical of Chianti, surrounded by lawns dotted with flower-beds and terracotta urns. The thick walls and stone windows are designed to keep out the intense summer sun and an astute use of space and simple white walls prevents any sensation of gloominess.

Most of the furniture in the common areas and bedrooms is rustic antique with a few non-intrusive modern pieces; those in the older building are more characteristic. The whole place is watched over by a professional and attentive staff. Breakfast is the only meal served but there is no shortage of good restaurants in the vicinity.

Nearby Siena (21 km); San Gimignano (31 km); Florence (45 km).

Via Fiorentina, Castellina in Chianti, 53011 Siena
Tel (0577) 740484
Fax (0577) 740998
Location 500m outside town, on road to San Donato in Poggio; own grounds; ample car parking
Meals breakfast
Prices L-LL
Rooms 19 double, all with bath or shower, phone
Facilities sitting-room, breakfast-room, gardens, swimming-pool
Smoking allowed
Credit cards MC, V
Children welcome
Disabled one adapted room
Pets not accepted
Closed never
Languages English, German, French
Proprietor Angela Orlandi

Siena

Tenuta di Ricavo

Like Tuscan cooking, the secret of Tenuta di Ricavo's success is easy to describe but difficult to reproduce: simple local ingredients of the highest quality, artfully combined. Here at Ricavo, all the essential elements are present: a hamlet of small stone houses strung out along a hillside, attentive Swiss-Italian owners, and the well-tried formula of a country hotel in the heart of Chianti. The centre of the hamlet is a gravel piazza divided along the diagonal by a row of cypresses. On one side is the main house which now contains the restaurant, sitting-rooms and some of the bedrooms. On the other side of the cypresses are the former farm buildings and peasant dwellings. The hamlet stretches back some distance, so there is no danger of guests crowding in on one another. Furnishing and decoration are of the highest standards. Bedrooms in the main house are more spacious and formal; the others have more individual character, and many have terraces looking on to the wooded valley. The bathrooms have all been recently re-done, and there is a new swimming-pool. One of the finest hotels in the Chianti region – and with a top-class restaurant too.

Nearby Siena (22 km); Florence (45 km).

Loc. Ricavo 4, Castellina in Chianti 53011 Siena
Tel (0577) 740221
Fax (0577) 741014
Location 1 km N of Castellina in Chianti in own grounds; ample car parking
Meals breakfast, lunch, dinner
Prices LL-LLL;
Rooms 2 single, 13 double, 8 suites all with bath or shower, phone; TV, safe, minibar; 3-day minimum stay in high season

Facilities sitting-rooms, bar, restaurant, terrace, 2 swimming-pools, table tennis, gym **Smoking** not in dining-room **Credit cards** MC, V **Children** quiet ones **Disabled** no special facilities; some rooms on ground floor **Pets** not accepted **Closed** Nov to Easter; restaurant only Tue, Wed; Mon-Thu lunch (summer) **Languages** English, French, German **Proprietor** Christina Lobrano-Scotoni

Siena

Country villa, Castellina in Chianti

Villa Casalecchi

This 18thC villa stands on a series of hillside terraces between woods and vineyards, just south of Castellina. The house is no architectural gem, but its secluded position and attractive location compensate for a certain austerity of style in the exteriors. Originally used as a hunting lodge (witness the hallway hung with trophies), the interiors are furnished with heavy, bourgeois antiques which give a hushed character that you might expect visiting the home of an eminent Victorian. The dining-room is frescoed with elegant old light fittings, but a more pleasant place to eat is the terrace with its views of open countryside. Bedrooms are either in the villa (individually furnished), or in the extension, with access to the gardens and pool. Parquet floors and a lighter style of antique makes them more convivial than the public rooms.

The terraces are attractive and well-tended, exploiting their prime location. Some are dotted with flower-filled pots. Down a level is the swimming-pool and below that another terrace, on the edge of the vineyard, where you can lie on a comfortable sun bed. For the energetic, the glories of Chianti are on the doorstep.
Nearby Florence (40 km); Siena (20 km).

Loc. Casalecchi, Castellina in Chianti, 53011 Siena
Tel (0577) 740240
Fax (0577) 741111
Location one km S of Castellina in own grounds; ample car parking
Meals breakfast, lunch, dinner
Prices LL-LLL
Rooms 23 double, all with shower or bath, phone, TV
Facilities sitting-rooms, breakfast-room, dining-room, bar, swimming-pool, tennis-court, bowls
Smoking allowed
Credit cards AE, DC, EC, MC, V
Children welcome
Disabled no special facilities
Pets accepted but not in public rooms
Closed Oct to Mar
Languages English, French, German
Proprietor Elvira Lecchini-Giovannoni

Siena

Hilltop village, Castelnuovo Berardenga

Relais Borgo San Felice

Larger than most of the entries in the guide, Borgo San Felice can legitimately be included because this carefully renovated hilltop hamlet is like a collection of charming small hotels. Surrounded by cypresses and the vineyards of the renowned San Felice estate, the tranquil village has the air of being suspended in time. No intrusive neon signs, no lines of cars, just the original Tuscan qualities of perfectly proportioned space setting off simple buildings of brick and stone and topped by a jumble of terracotta roofs. Even the swimming-pool (which can often resemble a gaping, blue gunshot wound) has been discreetly tucked away. Gravel paths, carved well-heads, pergolas, lemon trees in gigantic terracotta pots, a church, a bell-tower and a chapel – one is in the presence of the essence of Tuscany.

All the original features of the various buildings have been retained: vaulted brick ceilings, imposing fireplaces, old tiled floors. The furniture is a stylish mixture of old and modern and the sitting-rooms are full of intimate alcoves. An elegant restaurant completes the picture. Top of the range – and so are the prices.
Nearby Siena (21 km).

Loc. Borgo San Felice,
Castelnuovo Berardenga
53019 Siena
Tel (0577)359260
Fax (0577)359089
Location 21km NE of Siena
in former estate village;
ample car parking
Meals breakfast, lunch,
dinner
Prices rooms LLL-LLLL
Rooms 12 suites, 36 double,
7 single; all with bath or
shower, phone, TV, minibar

Facilities swimming-pool,
tennis courts, bowls court,
billiards room, conference
rooms, sitting-rooms
Smoking permitted
Credit cards AE, DC, MC, V
Children welcome
Disabled one suitable room
but access in general difficult
Pets small dogs
Closed Nov to March
Languages English
Manager Lorenzo Righi

Siena

Farm guest-house, Castelnuovo Berardenga

Podere San Quirico

Guests receive a real Neapolitan welcome from Maria Consiglio Picone. The first thing she did when we arrived, on a hot July day, was rush into her kitchen and make us some some freshly squeezed peach juice. From that moment on, she could do no wrong.

The house is a slightly battered relic from the 14thC, built of the local light-coloured stone, with an arched entrance and small, brown-shuttered windows. Terracotta pots filled with flowering plants are dotted about the forecourt where there are also seats to relax in. Perhaps because of Maria's Neapolitan origins and career as a theatre costume designer, the interiors are decorated with more vivacity than is usual in this part of Tuscany: the walls are festooned with plates and paintings, and a lifetime's collection of bric-a-brac cheerfully clutters up the space.

The bedrooms are less festive but enlivened with colourful fabrics and old rugs strewn on the terracotta floors. Bathrooms are up to the mark. Guest can eat in the numerous restaurants or pizzeria nearby or, if they prefer, a separate kitchen and dining-room is at their disposal. And to do? "Here, we sell silence," says Maria.
Nearby Siena (20 km).

Via del Paradiso 1
Castelnuovo Berardenga,
53019 Siena
Tel (0577) 355206
Fax (0577) 355206
Location 20 km E of Siena,
just outside Castelnuovo
Berardenga, in own grounds;
car parking
Meals breakfast on request
Prices L
Rooms 7 double all with
private bathroom; 2
apartments, for 3 or 5 people

(L-LL)
Facilities breakfast-room,
garden with barbecue,
kitchen/dining-room
Smoking preferably not
Credit cards not accepted
Children welcome (free for
under-fives)
Disabled not suitable
Pets not accepted
Closed never
Languages English
Proprietor Maria Consiglio
Picone

Siena

Country villa, Castelnuovo Berardenga

Villa Curina

A vivacious, convivial atmosphere pervades this hotel-and-apartment complex set in low, rolling countryside north of Siena; when we visited, it was full of activity with people enjoying themselves in the pool, playing tennis or going out for bike rides. In fact, some may find it too energetic for their requirements.

The main villa, surrounded by ornamental gardens and trees, is a large, cream-coloured, 18thC building and contains the bedrooms for guests as well as the principal public rooms. Most of the apartments are in three old stone farmhouses with small, brown-shuttered windows and connected by pathways of Siena brick. The bedrooms are furnished in a slightly heavier version of the standard rustic manner, but they are all comfortable and well-lit. An attractive restaurant, spanned by strong brick arches, serves fresh produce from the estate along with its own wine and grappa.

Terraced gardens covered with a profusion of flowers and geometric box-hedges lead down from the side of the villa to the swimming-pool and its large, terracotta-paved solarium. A quieter, shadier gravel terrace can be found at the back.

Nearby Castelnuovo Berardenga (6 km); Siena (20 km).

Loc. Curina, Castelnuovo Berardenga, 53019 Siena
Tel (0577) 355586
Fax (0577) 355412
Location 6 km W of Castelnuovo Berardenga in its own grounds; ample car parking
Meals breakfast, dinner
Prices L-LL
Rooms 12 doubles, all with bath or shower, phone, TV; 13 apartments for 2-6 persons

Facilities restaurant, terrace, gardens, bikes, swimming-pool, tennis,
Smoking not in the restaurant
Credit cards EC, MC, V
Children welcome
Disabled no special facilities
Pets not accepted
Closed Nov to Mar/Apr
Languages English, German
Manager Franco Sbardelati

Siena

Former convent, Cetona

La Frateria

One of the more unusual entries in this guide and not a hotel in the strict sense but a place of hospitality run by a community that has withdrawn from the world. The buildings, grouped around a hillside church founded in 1212 by St. Francis, constructed out of light, golden stone, form a rambling complex. Only seven rooms and suites are available, so, even when it is fully booked, one never has the sensation of being in a busy hotel but a place of retreat. There is no swimming-pool and none of the rooms has a television.

This may sound monastic, but the setting and furnishings are of the same standard as a top-class hotel: antiques, paintings and colourful wooden carvings (generally religious in theme) and spacious rooms with stone and beige stucco walls. The restaurant is unexpectedly sophisticated (and expensive), serving a mixture of refined and hearty food using fresh produce from the gardens.

A stroll around the monastery with its church and chapel, cloisters and courtyards, and hushed, tranquil air will help you realize why the young people of this community want to share their peace.

Nearby Pienza (40 km); Montepulciano (26 km); Montalcino (6 km); Siena (89 km).

Convento di San Francesco, Cetona, 53040 Siena
Tel (0578) 238015
Fax (0578) 239220
Location restored monastery 26 km S of Montepulciano in own grounds; ample car parking
Meals breakfast, lunch, dinner
Prices LLLL
Rooms 5 double, 2 suites, all with bath or shower, heating

Facilities sitting-rooms, restaurant, terrace, garden
Smoking permitted
Credit cards AE, EC, MC, V
Children welcome
Disabled no special facilities
Pets not accepted
Closed Jan; restaurant only, Tue in winter
Languages English
Manager Maria Grazia Daolio

Siena

Hilltop castle, Gaiole in Chianti

Castello di Spaltenna

A dramatically situated, fortified monastery on a hilltop next to the medieval church of Santa Maria di Spaltenna. Constructed from hewn stone with towers at each corner, the castle is built around a central courtyard with creeper-clad walls. Its genial Irish proprietor, Seamus de Pentheny O'Kelly, left recently to start up a new restaurant in Brolio, and the place is under new ownership and management. We have heard that standards may not be the same as under the old management. Reports would be welcome.

Meals are served either in the swish restaurant or in the courtyard. No effort has been spared in making the hotel a paragon of taste and refinement. No two bedrooms are the same: antiques, four-poster beds and the imaginative use of fabrics designed by Seamus's wife, Julia, add a lively touch to the medieval architecture.

In the past we've had reports from readers who felt that the price is not justified by the standard of service, but maybe they struck off days: our latest visit makes us think that it is one of the best hotels in the Chianti area, and well worth the expense.
Nearby Siena (28 km); Florence (45 km).

Gaiole in Chianti, 53013
Siena
Tel (0577) 749483
Fax (0577) 749269
Location on hilltop just outside Gaiole, 28 km NE of Siena; car parking
Meals breakfast, lunch, dinner
Prices LL-LLL-LLLL
Rooms 17 double, 4 suites, all with bath or shower, phone, TV, minibar, air-conditioning
Facilities sitting-rooms, restaurant, courtyard terrace, wine bar, garden, swimming-pool with cascade, walks, fishing; cookery courses
Smoking allowed
Credit cards AE, DC, EC, MC, V **Children** welcome
Disabled no special facilities
Pets small dogs, small charge
Closed 20 Nov to 20 Mar
Languages English, French German, Portuguese
Manager Jeancarlo Bellomini

Siena

Country apartments, Gaiole in Chianti

Castello di Tornano

One of the countless defence and watch towers that dot Tuscany, solidly built of grey stone in positions with commandng views of the surrounding countryside, many of them in line of sight with their neighbours. Here, you find yourself in one of the wilder parts of Chianti with views of steep wooded hills, bleak in winter and, even in summer, with an air of inviolable isolation.

Most of the apartments are in a farmhouse adjoining the base of the thousand-year-old tower, and each has a living room with a kitchen area, and one or two bedrooms, furnished in a rustic style, deployed in a relatively simple manner. Some of the apartments are in the tower, and these are decorated with a more studied elegance. Each has its own entrance and a private outdoor area.

The swimming-pool is in a common area and, fittingly for the location, has been fashioned from the remains of the former moat, still spanned by a wooden bridge. Nearby is a small fishing lake and, at the bottom of the hill, a typical Tuscan *trattoria*. Produce from the estate (wine, oil, vinegar, cheese, eggs and salami) can be bought on the spot.

Nearby Siena (16 km); Florence (50 km).

Loc. Lecchi, Gaiole in Chianti, 53013 Siena
Tel (0577) 746067;
 (055) 6580918 (bookings)
Fax (0577) 746067;
 (055) 6580918 (bookings)
Location 5 km S of Gaiole; own grounds, ample car parking
Meals self-catering apartments; family *trattoria* nearby
Prices L-LL
Rooms 9 fully equipped

apartments for 2-6 persons
Facilities bar, gardens; cleaners on request; swimming-pool , tennis
Smoking permitted
Credit cards AE, DC
Children welcome
Disabled not suitable
Pets small, on request
Closed Nov to Mar
Languages English, French, some German
Manager Barbara Sevolini

Siena

Country village hotel, Lecchi in Chianti

San Sano

The medieval hamlet of San Sano, a clutter of stone houses with uneven terracotta roofs, has at its heart an ancient defence tower, destroyed and rebuilt many times. Now, in its latest incarnation, this imposing structure forms the core of a delightful, family-run hotel in a relatively little visited, authentic part of Chianti.

The various buildings surrounding the tower (which houses some of the bedrooms; others have direct access to the grounds) give the hotel a rambling character, connected by narrow passage-ways, steep stairways and unexpected courtyards. The restoration has been meticulous and restrained. The decoration is in classic, rustic Tuscan style but with individual touches: carefully chosen antiques, colourful pottery and plenty of flowers. The dining-room, in the former stables, spanned by a massive stone arch and still with the feeding trough, is a cool haven from the summer sun. Each bedroom has its individual character (one with nesting birds in its perforated walls, now glassed off) and gleaming, almost surgical bathrooms. Outside is a stone-paved garden at the foot of the tower and, at a slight remove, a hillside swimming-pool.

Nearby Radda in Chianti (9 km); Siena (25 km); Florence (60 km).

Loc. San Sano, Lecchi in Chianti, 53010 Siena
Tel (0577) 746130
Fax (0577) 746156
Location hill-top hamlet in middle of countryside; own car parking
Meals breakfast, dinner
Prices LL
Rooms 11 doubles, 2 single, all with bath or shower, phone, central heating
Facilities sitting-areas, breakfast and dining-room, garden, swimming-pool
Smoking not allowed in some public areas
Credit cards AE, DC, EC, MC, V **Children** welcome
Disabled one adapted room; ground-floor rooms accessible
Pets please check first
Closed mid-Nov to mid-Mar
Languages English, German, French, Spanish
Proprietors Giancarlo and Heidi Matarazzo

Siena

La Chiusa

Quite a few of the better small hotels in this guide started off as restaurants and over the years have converted a few rooms for overnight visitors, with such success that they have extended this side of their activities. But in general it is true to say that the restaurant remains the centre of the enterprise. Not that at La Chiusa, a stone farmhouse and *frantoio* (olive-press), the comfort of guests is secondary. The greatest care and attention has been given to the bedrooms and suites: elegant and spacious, each has been individually furnished with antiques. Colourful rugs cover the old terracotta tiles and modern lamps provide artful lighting. Bathrooms are among the best we have seen, some with hydro-massage and one incorporating old millstones.

Dania Masotti is justifiably proud of her achievements as a cook, and meals in the elegant (and pricey) restaurant are gastronomic experiences that venture beyond the merely regional, despite being based on home ingredients from the farm and vegetable garden. Even the bread served at breakfast is baked on the premises. Extensive gardens, filled with fragrant rosemary and lavender.

Nearby Montepulciano (10 km); Pienza (10 km).

Via della Madonnina 88,
Montefollonico, 53040 Siena
Tel (0577) 669668
Fax (0577) 669593
Location 10 km NW of
Montepulciano; in own
grounds, ample car parking
Meals breakfast, lunch,
dinner
Prices LLL-LLLL
Rooms 6 double, 5 suites, all
with bath, phone, TV,
minibar; 3 apartments

Facilities sitting-room,
restaurant, garden
Smoking allowed
Credit cards AE, DC, EC, MC,
V **Children** welcome
Disabled one adapted room
Pets accepted
Closed Jan to Mar; restaurant
only, Jan to Mar, Tue
Languages English, French,
German
Proprietors Dania Masotti
and Umberto Lucherini

Siena

Village hotel, Monteriggioni

Monteriggioni

Visitors to Tuscany have been increasingly keen to drop by well-preserved, medieval Monteriggioni and spend a couple of hours relaxing in the piazza (where a bar serves snacks), browsing the antique shops or sampling the menu of Il Pozzo, one of the finest restaurants in the Siena area. Finally, somebody had the bright idea that a small hotel would not go amiss, especially since the town is peaceful and well placed for exploring the locality.

A couple of old stone houses were knocked together and converted with sure-handed lightness of touch to make this attractive hotel. The former stables now make a large, light and airy public area used as reception, sitting-room and breakfast-room.

At the back, a door leads out to a well-tended garden running down to the town walls and containing what it possibly the smallest swimming-pool in Tuscany. The bedrooms are perfectly acceptable, furnished to a high rustic-antique standard with stylish hyper-modern bathrooms.

Nearby Siena (10 km); San Gimignano (18 km); Florence (55 km); Volterra (40 km).

Via 1 Maggio 4,
Monteriggioni, 53035 Siena
Tel (0577) 305009, 305010
Fax (0577) 305011
Location within the walls
of Monteriggioni, 10 km N of
Siena; car parking available
outside the walls
Meals breakfast
Prices LL-LLL
Rooms 2 single, 10 double,
all with bath or shower,
phone, TV, minibar,
air-conditioning

Facilities sitting area,
breakfast-room, bar, garden,
small swimming-pool
Smoking permitted
Credit cards AE, DC, EC, MC,
V
Children welcome
Disabled no special facilities
Pets accepted, but check first
Closed Jan to Feb
Languages English, French,
German
Manager Michela Gozzi

Siena

Country hotel, Monteriggioni

San Luigi

There has been no skimping or cutting corners in the conversio of the farm buildings of San Luigi to a country hotel with a diffen ence, which we think will appeal to some readers, especially thos travelling with a young family. A long, unpaved drive takes yo through acres of grounds to the main building and receptior When we remarked on how green everything was, even in summe we learned that this was originally an Etruscan settlement and tha they always chose areas with supplies of underground water.

Certainly, the present owners of San Luigi have exploited th lush setting. The park is crammed with things to do: swimmin; tennis, volleyball, basketball, bowls, even a giant chessboard. If liv ly group activity is not for you, there are acres of countryside fo rambles and secluded corners to retreat to with a book.

It would be unfair to describe San Luigi as a holiday camp, but would be equally misleading to recommend it to readers in searc of a tranquil break. Guests, when we visited, seemed incredib active – especially the younger generation – and copious buffe meals helped to fuel their energies.

Nearby Monteriggioni (5 km); Siena (12 km); Florence (50 km).

Loc. Strove, Via della Cerreta 38, Monteriggioni, 53030 Siena
Tel (0577) 301055
Fax (0577) 301167
Location 5 km NW of Monteriggioni in its own spacious park; ample car parking
Meals breakfast, lunch, dinner
Prices LL-LLL, all with bath or shower, minibar
Rooms 2 single, 32 double, 5 apartments for 2-6 people, all with bath or shower
Facilities sitting-room, restaurant, bar, gardens, tennis, volley- and basket-ball, 2 swimming-pools, giant chess
Smoking permitted
Credit cards AE, DC, EC, MC, V **Children** welcome
Disabled no special facilities
Pets small dogs accepted
Closed never
Languages English, French, German
Proprietor Sig. Michelagnoli

Siena

Former monastery, Pienza

Il Chiostro di Pienza

In the modest way of Renaissance popes, Pius II re-named his home town of Corsignano after himself and made it a model of 15thC urban planning. So it is appropriate that the modern tourist-pilgrim should find lodgings in this stylishly converted monastery. The entrance is located at the back of the austere white cloister that gives the hotel its name and on to which half the rooms look; the other half face away, over the serenely magnificent hills of Val d'Orcia.

Many of the original features of the monks' cells have been retained: frescoed, vaulted ceilings and tiled floors. The furniture, however, breaks with monkish antiquity and concentrates on modern comfort without sinning against the character of the building. Bathrooms, though hardly spacious, are fully equipped.

The sitting-rooms, with their old beamed ceilings, and the restaurant, give on to a delightful terrace garden. There could be no more agreeable place for one's evening *aperitivo* than its tranquil shade before strolling down Pienza'a elegant Corso to the many restaurants around.

Nearby Palazzo Piccolomini, the Cathedral; Siena (52 km).

Corso Rossellino 26, Pienza, 53026 Siena
Tel (0578) 748400
Fax (0578) 748440
Location centre of town next to Palazzo Piccolomini
Meals breakfast, lunch, dinner
Prices rooms LL-LLL
Rooms 25 double, 2 single, 2 suites; all with bath; all rooms have phone, TV
Facilities sitting-rooms, bar, restaurant, garden
Smoking permitted
Credit cards AE, DC, MC, V
Children welcome
Disabled access difficult
Pets not accepted
Closed Nov to March
Languages English
Manager Michela Boneface

Siena

Country hotel, Pienza

La Saracina

It seems to us that, when 'foreigners' buy country houses in Italy to turn into guest-houses, they sometimes make a better job of it than Italians themselves – or, perhaps taking less for granted, they understand what appeals to non-Italian visitors. Such is the case of La Saracina run by the McCobbs who, through hard work and attention to detail, have turned this farmhouse into something special.

The location, of course, helps: it has a view of seven towns, and the countryside is glorious. But the McCobbs have built on their good fortune and added to it their own refinement and taste. The bedrooms are spacious and elegant with luxurious bathrooms fitted with hydro-massage baths and marble sinks. Antique furnishings combine well with the bright fabrics, and each room has independent access. The suites also have their own sitting areas.

Breakfast (which includes local hams and cheeses, and muffins) is served on the terrace in fine weather or else in a neat breakfast-room. There is an attractive swimming-pool. More expensive than most guest-houses, but La Saracina offers a little more too.
Nearby Pienza (7 km); Montepulciano (6 km).

Strada Statale 146, Pienza,
53026 Siena
Tel (0578) 748022
Fax (0578) 748022
Location on quiet hillside
outside Pienza; car parking
Meals breakfast
Prices LL-LLL
Rooms 1 double, 3 suites,
1 apartment (with kitchen),
all with bath or shower,
phone, TV
Facilities breakfast-room,
garden, swimming-pool,
tennis
Smoking permitted
Credit cards AE, EC, MC, V
Children welcome
Disabled access difficult
Pets not accepted
Closed never
Languages English, Spanish
Proprietors Donald and
Jessie McCobb

Siena

Country villa, Pievescola di Casole d'Elsa

Relais La Suvera

1507, when Siena gave the castle of Suvera to Pope Julius II, he
⎯ded an entire Renaissance villa on the same scale. Later, it
⎯anged hands many times (belonging once to the film director,
⎯sconti); now it is one of the most extraordinary hotels in Italy.
⎯Stone-built and three storeys high, in a panoramic position, the
⎯ncompromising lines of the fortress wing contrast with the deli-
⎯te arched loggias, the villa's principal façade. To the side stands a
⎯thC church, and ornamental gardens carved up by precisely
⎯gned gravel paths.
⎯To do justice to the interiors would require a book in itself. A
⎯llector's fantasies come true? A display of aristocratic luxury? Or
⎯ essay in kitsch? Each room has a theme (the Pope's Room, the
⎯oor's Room, the Ceramics Room) and each theme has been pur-
⎯ed to its limits. Napoleon's Room is furnished in pure Empire
⎯yle, hung with heavy drapes and contains a portrait of the brood-
⎯g megalomaniac himself, surmounted by an Imperial Eagle.
⎯ooms in the converted stables are (relatively) simpler and small-
⎯. An elegant restaurant occupies the former olive-press.
⎯earby Siena (28 km); Florence (56 km).

Loc. Pievescola di Casole
d'Elsa, 53030 Siena
Tel (0577) 960 300/1/2/3
Fax (0577) 960 220
Location 28 km W of Siena,
in its own grounds; car
parking
Meals breakfast, lunch,
dinner
Prices LLL-LLLL
Rooms 23 doubles, 12 suites,
all with bath or shower, TV,
phone, air-conditioning
Facilities sitting-rooms,

breakfast-room, restaurant,
swimming-pool, tennis
Smoking permitted
Credit cards AE, DC, EC,
MC, V
Children small children
welcome
Disabled not suitable
Pets not accepted
Closed Nov to Mar
Languages English, French,
German, Spanish
Proprietor Marchese Ricci

Siena

Country villa, Poggibonsi

Villa San Lucchese

Do not be put off by nearby Poggibonsi, which, most people agree
is one of the ugliest towns in Tuscany. Lying halfway between
Florence and Siena, visitors take one look at it from the motorway
and speed on, or are forced to skirt it on the way to San
Gimignano. However, its ugliness is contained, and once outside its
environs, you are back in glorious Tuscan countryside, conscious
only of cypresses, olives and vines – which is what you will also see
from Villa San Lucchese's hilltop.

The villa is an elegant, 15thC cream-coloured building standing
in its own park of sculpted hedges and swirling gravel paths. The
interiors have been extensively refurbished to the standards of a
four-star hotel, with perhaps more attention paid to modern comforts than to original style. Still, plenty of the character of the old
villa remains, whether in the reception area with its heavy-beamed
ceilings and low arches or in the dining-room's friezes and sloping
roof. More colour would have been welcome in the bedrooms
which, with their predominantly white tones, lacked vivacity and
personality, even if spacious and comfortable.

Nearby Siena (19 km); Florence (36 km); San Gimignano (13 km)

Via San Lucchese 5,
Poggibonsi, 53036 Siena
Tel (0577) 934231
Fax (0577) 934729
Location 2 km S of
Poggibonsi on hilltop in
own grounds; car parking
Meals breakfast, lunch,
dinner
Prices LL-LLL
Rooms 31 double, 2 suites, all
with bath or shower, TV,
phone, minibar, air-
conditioning

Facilities sitting-rooms,
restaurant, bar, garden, two
swimming-pools, tennis
courts, bowls
Smoking allowed
Credit cards AE, EC, MC, V
Children welcome
Disabled no special facilities
Pets not accepted
Closed Nov to Mar
Languages English, French
Manager Gianfranco
Innocenti

Siena

Country hotel, Radda in Chianti

Relais Fattoria Vignale

attoria Vignale is not only in the heart of Chianti, it was here that 1924, Baldassare Pianigiani created the famous black rooster mbol and the Consorzio Vino Chianti Classico, which to this day ts the standards for the production of Italy's most famous wine.

The hotel also sets high standards for itself. Under the management of the quietly efficient Silvia Kummer, you should find no nexpected hitches during your stay here. Decoration and furnishing are tasteful and restrained and blend well with the original haracter of the manor house. The sitting-rooms are subdued in haracter, with elegant modern sofas and Persian rugs. One is decrated with frescoed panels depicting rural scenes. The bedrooms, ncluding the ones in the annex across the road, are all well furished in a superior rustic style.

The building is situated on a slope, and while the front resembles a town house, the back, a couple of levels down, is more like a rmhouse. Here, under a leafy pergola, breakfast is served, and a ttle further away, with the same dramatic views, is the swimming-ool. Everything we look for in a charming small hotel.

earby Siena (28 km); San Gimignano (40 km); Firenze (45 km).

Via Pianigiani 15, Radda in Chianti, 53017 Siena
Tel (0577) 738300
Fax (0577) 738592
Location just outside village, 28 km N of Siena; own grounds, ample car parking
Meals breakfast, snacks
Prices LL-LLL
Rooms 25 double, 4 single, all with bath or shower, phone, TV, heating. 9 of the rooms are in the annex across the road

Facilities 3 sitting-rooms, breakfast-room, bar, terrace, garden, swimming-pool
Smoking non-smoking breakfast-room
Credit cards AE, EC, MC, V
Children welcome but preferably quiet ones
Disabled lift, but no special facilities **Pets** not accepted
Closed 8th-26th Dec; 6th Jan-25th Mar **Languages** English, German, French
Manager Silvia Kummer

Siena

Country guest-house, Radda in Chianti

Podere Terreno

At Podere Terreno you will find everything you might expect from a family guest-house in the heart of Chianti: a four-hundred-year old farmhouse with views of vines and olive groves; delicious home cooking; and a genuinely friendly welcome.

The dining-room on the upper floor is the centre of the house. As well as eating meals together at the long wooden table, guest can relax in front of the huge, traditional fireplace, its wooden mantle hung with cheerful ceramics and mounted antlers. The room is packed full of rural artifacts: burnished copper vessel hang from the wooden beams, a cupboard hollowed out of a tree trunk, shelves stacked with bottles of wine. Downstairs there another sitting-room. The bedrooms, all off a long corridor, are simply but well furnished, each named after a type of vine, the white plaster walls enlivened with coloured stencils of flowers and plants. Bathrooms are smallish, with slightly garish green tiling.

Come evening, you can take your glass of red to the covered sitting area in the garden and watch the swallows swirling around the terracotta roofs.

Nearby Siena (35 km); Florence (43 km).

Via Terreno 21, Volpaia,
Radda in Chianti, 53017
Siena
Tel (0577) 738312
Fax (0577) 738312
Location 5 km N of Radda in
Chianti; car parking
Meals breakfast, dinner
Prices LL (DB&B); 2-day
minimum stay
Rooms 7 double, 6 with
shower, 1 with bath
Facilities sitting-room, dining-
room, terrace, table-tennis;
lake nearby
Smoking not at table
Credit cards AE, EC, MC, V
Children welcome
Disabled not suitable
Pets accepted
Closed never
Languages English, French,
German
Proprietors Marie-Sylvie
Haniez and Roberto Melosi

Siena

Vescine - Il Relais del Chianti

There is an almost manicured air to the buildings and gardens of Vescine, a group of perfectly-restored farmhouses strung out along a hillside between Castellina and Radda. Perhaps it is because of the comparatively recent restructuring in 1990 that these medieval buildings look as if they might be a film set. Everything is in perfect order: not a tile out of place, not a weed in the garden. The sitting-rooms are on two levels of an upper floor connected by a stone stairway. The lower one is spacious, with exposed beam ceilings supported by a large white column that divides the room up into various areas including a bar; the upper one is smaller and rather pretentiously called a library on the strength of a few books.

The bedrooms are spread around the various houses (which are connected by brick paths, criss-crossing the terraced gardens) and are in the same pristine style. A little more imagination and fewer hackneyed pictures would have given them more character.

The location of the hotel provides it with panoramic views, especially from the swimming-pool. The restaurant is some distance away and there are plenty of others in the area.

Nearby Siena (28 km); Florence (42 km).

Loc. Vescine, Radda in Chianti, 53017 Siena
Tel (0577) 741144
Fax (0577) 740263
Location 5 km E of Castellina, just off road to Radda; own grounds, ample car parking
Meals breakfast; associated restaurant 700m away
Prices LLL-LLLL
Rooms 16 double, 7 suites, all with bath or shower, phone, TV, minibar
Facilities sitting-room, bar, breakfast-room, garden, tennis, swimming-pool
Smoking allowed
Credit cards AE, EC, MC, V
Children welcome
Disabled no special facilities
Pets dogs accepted
Closed Nov to Mar
Languages English, French, German
Manager Birgit Fleig

Siena

Country guest-house, Radicofani

La Palazzina

La Palazzina was once a restaurant with a few rooms, but it is now a guest-house with the bonus of excellent in-house dining. Certainly the setting is too attractive only to use for a few hours in the evening : a 17thC hilltop hunting lodge approached by an alley of cypresses in rolling countryside, with manicured gardens and a pristine swimming-pool.

The interiors are more modern than the house's 17thC origins would lead you to expect, and are due to an unfortunate restructuring by a previous owner. But not all character has been lost and much has been added, through the judicious use of 19thC antiques and stylishly chosen fabrics. Black-and-white tiling on the floors makes a welcome change from terracotta and gives a clean, cool look to the rooms. The bedrooms are in a similar style with beamed ceilings and wrought-iron beds; a few have their own terraces.

The restaurant is still an important part of life at La Palazzina, using fresh produce from the farm. The cuisine rises above the level of 'local specialities', and is served to softly playing baroque music in the elegant restaurant.

Nearby Pienza; Montepulciano (30 km); Montalcino (35 km).

Loc. Le Vigne, Celle sul Rigo, Radicofani, 53040 Siena	**Facilities** sitting-room, bar, restaurant, garden, swimming-pool; riding nearby
Tel (0578) 55771	
Fax (0578) 53553	**Smoking** allowed
Location 5 km E of Radicofani in its own grounds; ample car parking	**Credit cards** AE, EC, MC, V
	Children welcome
	Disabled one adapted room
Meals breakfast, lunch, dinner	**Pets** not accepted
	Closed Nov to Mar
Prices LL (DB&B); half-board is obligatory	**Languages** English
	Proprietor Nicoletta Innocenti
Rooms 10 double, all with bath or shower; 2 apartments	

Siena

Country guest-house, San Gimignano

Casale del Cotone

n impressively restored farmhouse that has been decorated with
ste to make it one of the finer bed-and-breakfasts in the San
imignano area. The house, a long, low building with small brown-
uttered windows and the occasional external stairway, was once
ed as a hunting lodge and in the breakfast-room are the remains
a fresco depicting a deer in flight and a pheasant.

Great care has been taken with both the interiors and exteriors.
utside are well-tended gardens with gravel paths and neatly kept,
lourful flowerbeds, and the house is so positioned that even on a
rrid August evening you will catch a cool breeze sitting there.
ans are also afoot to construct a swimming-pool.

On the ground floor is the sitting-room and breakfast area; in
e weather, breakfast is served in the garden. We were impressed
th the furniture and decoration, using a few well-chosen antiques
set off the fine proportions of the rooms. The bedrooms have a
milar, uncluttered, tasteful ambience, conducive to the peaceful,
most hushed atmosphere. The Casale opened relatively recently,
we would welcome reports.

earby Siena (35 km); Florence (50 km); Volterra (28 km).

Loc. Cellole 59, San
Gimignano, 53037 Siena
Tel (0577) 943236, 941395
Location 2 km N of San
Gimignano on the road to
Certaldo; own grounds,
ample car parking
Meals breakfast, snacks
Prices L-LL
Rooms 6 double,
2 apartments, all with bath
and shower
Facilities sitting-room, bar,

garden
Smoking permitted
Credit cards not accepted
Children very young only
Disabled one suitable room
Pets not accepted
Closed Nov to Jan
Languages English, French
Proprietor Alessandro
Martelli

Siena

Country hotel, San Gimignano

Le Renaie

Le Renaie is the sister hotel of the nearby Villa San Paolo (pa
107) and in some ways might be considered the poor relation, wi
a more modest approach to furnishing and decoration, but wi
the advantage of lower prices. The building is no architectural ma
terpiece, but a typical example of a modern rustic construction
covered terrace framed by brick arches where, in fine weathe
breakfast and dinner are served; French windows that open direc
on to the private balconies belonging to some of the bedrooms.

Inside, modern terracotta flooring and cane furniture make fe
a light, fresh atmosphere. The restaurant, Da Leonetto, is popul
with locals (especially for large functions) but gets mixed notic
from reporters. Upstairs are the bedrooms which have a mixture
modern, built-in furniture and reproduction rustic.

Guests seem to appreciate the peaceful location, the full rang
of hotel services (including a swimming-pool and access to the te
nis court of Villa San Paolo) and the very reasonable prices. A us
ful place to base yourself for a few days if you are thinking of co
bining city touring with days by the swimming-pool.
Nearby San Gimignano (5 km); Siena (38 km); Volterra.

Loc. Pancole, San
Gimignano, 53037 Siena
Tel (0577) 955044
Fax (0577) 955126
Location 6 km N of San
Gimignano, off road to
Certaldo; private car parking
Meals breakfast, lunch,
dinner
Prices L-LL
Rooms 24 double, 1 single,
all with bath or shower,
phone, TV, air-conditioning,
safe, minibar

Facilities sitting-area,
restaurant, garden,
swimming-pool
Smoking permitted
Credit cards AE, DC, EC, MC,
V **Children** welcome; must be
accompanied at swimming-
pool
Disabled no special facilities
Pets not in public areas
Closed Nov
Languages English, German,
French
Proprietor Leonetto Sabatini

Siena

Country villa, San Gimignano

Villa San Paolo

There is an almost un-Tuscan feel to Villa San Paolo. Not, of course, from the surroundings of cypresses and olives, and with a view of San Gimignano from the swimming-pool: you are in no doubt about where you are. But the villa is not particularly Tuscan in style, and inside, a lightness of touch in the choice of colours and furnishings gives it a welcome individuality and freshness.

On the ground floor are the foyer and public rooms in a pleasant mixture of grey, green and white; modern cane furniture is mixed with antiques. Bedrooms are on the two floors above, and those just below the roof have smallish windows. A common style has been followed with colour co-ordination of carpets, furniture and fabrics. One criticism: in one or two of the bedrooms it may be time to change the carpets. Bathrooms are spanking new with attractive check tiling.

Outside are the well-tended gardens, with gravel paths skirted by curling box-hedges under tall umbrella pines. A small ornamental fountain gurgles soothingly. The swimming-pool has its own bar and a covered terrace where breakfast is served in fine weather.
Nearby San Gimignano (5 km); Siena (38 km).

Strada per Certaldo, San Gimignano, 53037 Siena
Tel (0577) 955100
Fax (0577) 955113
Website
http://www.tin.it/san_gimignano
Location 5 km N of San Gimignano on the road to Certaldo; private car parking
Meals breakfast, snacks
Prices LL-LLL
Rooms 18 double all with bath or shower, phone, TV, minibar, safe, air-conditioning
Facilities sitting-room, breakfast-room, bar, garden, swimming-pool, tennis
Smoking permitted
Credit cards AE, DC, EC, MC, V **Children** welcome
Disabled adapted rooms available
Pets not accepted
Closed 8 Jan to Feb/Mar
Languages English, French, German
Manager Remo Squarcia

Siena

Country villa, San Gusme

Villa Arceno

Villa Arceno originally served as a hunting lodge for a Tuscan noble family, but 'lodge' is too humble a word to describe this aristocratic building. A long private road winds through the thousand-hectare estate (which has many farmhouses converted into apartments) to the square, rigidly symmetrical villa with its overhanging eaves, surrounded by lawns, gravel paths and flower-filled terracotta urns. In front of the villa is a separate, walled park in the Romantic style, with shady paths leading down to a small lake.

Inside, a cool, elegant style prevails: off-white walls and vaulted ceilings contrast with the warmth of terracotta floors (strewn with Persian carpets), reproduction antique furniture and light yellow drapes. The atmosphere is formal, but not stiffly so: the highly professional staff make guests feel more than welcome.

Upstairs, the guest-rooms which are all light and spacious, have been individually decorated. Particularly attractive is the suite which has a bay of three arched windows. Some rooms have their own terraces. You should also ask to see the spiral stairway of the central tower that finishes in a roof-top gazebo.

Nearby Siena (30 km); Florence (90 km).

Loc. Arceno, San Gusme,
Castelnuovo Berardenga,
53010 Siena
Tel (0577) 359292
Fax (0577) 359276
Location 30 km NE of Siena
in its own estate; ample car
parking
Meals breakfast, lunch,
dinner
Prices LLL-LLLL
Rooms 16 double, all with
bath, phone, TV, mini-bar,
air-conditioning

Facilities sitting-rooms,
restaurant, gardens, tennis,
swimming-pool, bikes
Smoking not encouraged; not
allowed in restaurant
Credit cards AE, DC, EC, MC,
V **Children** no
Disabled not suitable
Pets small dogs, but check
first
Closed mid-Nov to mid-Mar
Languages English, French,
German
Proprietor Gualtiero Mancini

Siena

Castello di Ripa d'Orcia

From the road below, the castle-village of Ripa d'Orcia is dominated by a solid and imposing stone tower, but as you climb up the cypress-bordered road, you will see the jumble of small houses that cluster around the tower, like ducklings cleaving to their mother. Cars must be parked outside the crenellated portico (except to deposit and pick up luggage), leaving the medieval character of the fortress almost intact.

Would-be aggressors must have thought twice about making any assault. From the side of the River Orcia, the castle represents a formidable obstacle with its sheer walls and corner watchtower, from which there are some exceptional views. Accommodation and restaurant are in the less dramatically positioned houses close to the entrance. The lines of the buildings are severe without any surface decoration to relieve the eye. Inside, the large rooms are in elegant rustic style, somewhat under-furnished, with few pictures on the plain white walls. A pleasant *trattoria* occupies the ground floor of one of the houses, serving Sienese specialities on an attractive terrace.

Nearby Bagno Vignoni (5 km); Pienza (19 km); Montalcino (24 km).

Loc. Castiglione d'Orcia, San Quirico d'Orcia, 53023 Siena
Tel (0577) 897376
Fax (0577) 898038
Location 5 km SW of San Quirico d'Orcia in own grounds; ample car parking
Meals breakfast, lunch, dinner
Prices L-LL
Rooms 6 double, 1 single, all with bath or shower; apartments for 2 to 4 persons;

3-night min.
Facilities sitting-room, restaurant, bar, gardens
Smoking allowed
Credit cards not accepted
Children welcome
Disabled no special facilities
Pets not accepted
Closed Jan and Feb
Languages English, French
Proprietor Laura Aluffi

Siena

Country guest-house, Sarteano

Le Anfore

The vicinity of Sarteano and Cetona is still relatively little visited despite the unspoilt countryside and the presence of good places in which to stay and eat – people gravitate instead to the Pienza/Montepulciano area. Here, nonetheless, is a 'find': Le Anfore, at the end of a track, off the Sarteano-Chiusi road.

The hotel consists of an old farmhouse that has been restored to a high standard and decorated with taste and style. The public rooms are on the ground floor, with a sitting-room, restaurant and bar that lead naturally to each other through brick-spanned arches which are in turn echoed by the windows. Most of the bedrooms are upstairs and seem to have senseless names ('Atoll', 'Arranvanna') until you realize that they have been called after horses from the riding stables. Rooms are spacious, with highly polished dark parquet floors strewn with Persian carpets; a couple have their own sitting areas and fireplaces. Each has been individually furnished with rustic and not-so-rustic antiques. Bathrooms are stylishly tiled and illuminated.

Outdoors, there is plenty to do – swimming, tennis and riding.
Nearby Chianciano Terme (14 km); Montepulciano (22 km).

Via di Chiusi 30, Sarteano,
53047 Siena
Tel (0578) 265871
Fax (0578) 265969
Location off the road
between Chiusi and Sarteano;
in own grounds; car parking
Meals breakfast, dinner
Prices L-LL
Rooms 7 double, 3 suites, all
with bath or shower, phone,
minibar
Facilities sitting-room, bar,

restaurant, garden, swimming-
pool, tennis, riding
Smoking permitted
Credit cards EC, MC, V
Children welcome
Disabled no special facilities;
accessible ground-floor
bedroom
Pets please check first
Closed never
Languages little English
spoken
Manager Maurizio Pozielli

Siena

Certosa di Maggiano

Though it lies in the suburbs of Siena, this former Carthusian monastery – the oldest in Tuscany – has the benefit of its own large park and a luxuriously peaceful atmosphere. Although it is expensive, it is not swanky. The emphasis is on calm elegance and discreet service. A star of our all-Italy guide, we feel we can hardly ignore it here.

If the decoration of the bedrooms is disappointing, it is only because they do not live up to the ravishing public rooms. Guests can help themselves to drinks in the book-lined library, play backgammon or chess in a little ante-room or relax in the lovely sitting-room. The fact that this was formerly the family home of the hotel's cultured owners is reflected in the country house atmosphere, with fresh flower arrangements just about everywhere. Excellent modern *haute cuisine* dishes are served with some ceremony in the pretty dining-room, in the tranquil 14thC cloisters or under the arcades by the swimming-pool.

Bear in mind that you will have to explore Siena by bus – it's too far to walk, and parking is almost impossible in the centre.

Nearby Siena sights; San Gimignano (40 km); Florence (58 km).

Via Certosa 82, Siena 53100.
Tel (0577) 288180
Fax (0577) 288189
Location 1 km SE of city centre and Porta Romana; in gardens, with car parking opposite entrance and garage available
Meals breakfast, lunch, dinner
Prices rooms LLL; suites LLLL; meals L-LL
Rooms 5 double, 12 suites; all with bath; all have central

heating, TV, phone, radio
Facilities dining-room, bar, library, sitting-room; tennis, heated outdoor swimming-pool, heliport
Credit cards AE, DC, MC, V
Children accepted
Disabled access possible – 3 rooms on ground floor
Pets small dogs accepted, but not in dining-room
Closed never
Manager Margherita Grossi

Siena

Locanda dell'Amorosa

In a corner of the Siena province, which is not overburdened with quality hotels, the Locanda dell'Amorosa shines out. It is as romantic as it sounds: an elegant Renaissance villa-cum-village, within the remains of the 14thC walls.

The accommodation consists of apartments in the houses where peasants and farm-workers once lived, or in the bedrooms in the old family residence. They are cool, airy and pretty, with whitewashed walls, terracotta floors, antique furniture and Florentine curtains and bedspreads – as well as immaculate modern bathrooms.

The old stables, beamed and brick-walled, have been transformed into a delightful rustic (but pricey) restaurant serving modern interpretations of traditional Tuscan recipes, using ingredients from the estate, which also produces wine.

To complete the village, there is a little parish church with a lovely 15thC fresco of the Sienese school. With discreet, attentive service, the Locanda dell'Amorosa remains, in our view, a Mecca for romantics.

Nearby Siena (45 km); Arezzo (45 km); Chianti.

Sinalunga, 53048 Siena
Tel (0577) 679497
Fax (0577) 678216
Location 2 km S of Sinalunga, ample car parking
Meals breakfast, lunch, dinner
Prices rooms LLLL; suites LLLL; meals from LL
Rooms 12 double, 4 suites, all with bathroom; all rooms have central heating, phone, colour TV, minibar, air-conditioning
Facilities dining-room, sitting-room, bar
Credit cards AE, DC, MC, V
Children accepted
Disabled access difficult
Pets not accepted
Closed mid-Jan to end Feb; restaurant only, Mon, Tue
Manager Carlo Citterio

Siena

Hillside hamlet, Sovicille

Borgo Pretale

A long, winding, unsurfaced road through wooded hills brings you to this group of grey stone houses clustered around a massive 10thC watchtower. Local historians claim that it was part of a system of such towers, spread across the Sienese hills, all within line of sight, to communicate quickly any news of approaching invaders and to provide protection against their rampages. Nowadays, this civilized retreat offers a haven from the rampages of modern life.

Every detail has been considered in the restoration and decoration. The harshness of the medieval structure has been lessened by the use of well-chosen antiques, mellow lighting and rich, striped fabrics. A serenely beautiful 15thC carved wooden Madonna, bearing the Infant Christ, stands in a brick-framed niche.

Every bedroom contains a different blend of the same artful ingredients, each splendid in its own individual way, though we particularly liked those in the tower. The stylish restaurant serves a limited choice of dishes (but all well-prepared) and has an extensive wine list on which a *sommelier* can offer advice. And tucked away, close to the edge of the woods, is an inviting pool.

Nearby Siena (20 km); San Gimignano (28 km).

Loc. Pretale, Rosia Sovicille, 53018 Siena
Tel (0577) 345401
Fax (0577) 345625
Location 20 km SE of Siena on quiet hillside; own car parking
Meals breakfast,, lunch, dinner
Prices LL-LLL
Rooms 25 double, 1 suite, all with bath or shower, phone, TV, minibar, air-conditioning

Facilities sitting-room, restaurant, bar, garden, club house, swimming-pool, tennis, sauna, archery
Smoking permitted
Credit cards all
Children welcome
Disabled not suitable
Pets not accepted
Closed mid-Nov to mid-Mar
Languages English, French German
Proprietor Daniele Rizzardini

Siena

Borgo di Toiano

Most of the abandoned rural hamlets (*borgo*) that once house
small farming communities and have since been converted int
distinctive hotels were, for protection's sake, located on steep hi
or jumbled together behind secure walls. Borgo di Toiano, by co
trast, has a pleasant open aspect: a few old stone houses, superb
restored, spread out across acres of stone and terracotta terrace
with views over the flat, cultivated valley to low hills on the horizo

The terraces, to which many of the bedrooms have direct acces
are dotted with rosebeds, flower pots and wrought-iron garden fu
niture, so that breakfast can be enjoyed in the early morning su
The main public rooms also maintain a spacious, uncluttered fee
with fine antiques and old rugs contrasting with the pristi
restoration. Tapestries and modern paintings are set off nicely
the white walls and subtle lighting. The bedrooms maintain th
same mixture of rustic and modern with the emphasis on simplici
and comfort, and we particularly recommend those with views.

Below the main group of houses, on the last terrace of this sha
low-sloping location, is the swimming-pool.

Nearby Siena (12 km); San Gimignano (50 km).

Loc. Toiano, Sovicille, 53018
Siena
Tel (0577) 314639
Fax (0577) 314641
Location 12 km SW of Siena
in its own grounds; car
parking
Meals breakfast
Prices LL-LLL
Rooms 7 double, 3 suites, all
with shower or bath, phone,
TV, minibar, air-conditioning
Facilities sitting-room, bar,
terraces, garden, swimming-
pool
Smoking permitted
Credit cards AE, DC, EC, MC,
V
Children welcome; extra bed
in room free
Disabled some adapted
rooms with bathrooms
Pets accepted
Closed Nov to Mar
Languages English, French,
German
Manager Pierluigi Pagni

Perugia

Country guest-house, Asproli

La Palazzetta

At some point in the 1920s, La Palazzetta must have been an artistic colony, for in many parts of this complex, formed of a villa and its surrounding farmhouses, one comes across remnants of creative activity – especially in the main building, where people often ask to see the frescoes by Dottori & Balla. It is easy to understand what attracted artists to this place: the wonderful Umbrian light which La Palazzetta, with its vistas of rolling green hills, enjoys to the maximum and the sense of community one feels in this compact group of houses, almost a small village. Aids to hedonism include a fine swimming-pool and a restaurant, while for the energetic there are country walks. (In the restaurant, incidentally, one can see evidence of La Palazzetta's artistic tradition in the *trompe-l'oeil* fresco that covers an entire wall.)

Furnishing and decor are of a good standard, although we did not get the opportunity to see the bedrooms in the main villa, said to be a cut above the others, some of which are a bit on the small side. Care has been taken in restoration not to disturb the native character of the original 17thC buildings.

Nearby Todi (8 km); Orvieto (30 km).

Loc. Asproli, Todi
06050 Perugia
Tel (075) 8853219
Fax (075) 8853358
Location 8 km SW of Todi, following signs on SS 448, in its own grounds; car parking.
Meals breakfast, lunch, dinner
Prices L
Rooms 19 double, all with bath or shower, phone, TV
Facilities sitting-room, bar, restaurant, garden, swimming-pool, bowls, archery, mountain bikes
Smoking permitted
Credit cards AE, EC, DC, MC, V **Children** welcome
Disabled no special facilities
Pets please check first
Closed Nov to mid-Feb (except Christmas)
Languages English, French German
Proprietor Ensoli Caracciolo Del Leone

Perugia

Country guest-house, Asproli

Poggio d'Asproli

If you are tired of Naples, you may not be tired of life – just in nee
of peace and quiet. Such was the case with Bruno Pagliari, so h
sold his large southern hotel to continue his career as an artist i
the tranquillity of Umbria's leafy valleys. But the tradition of hosp
tality remained, and he has opened up his hillside farmhouse s
that his guests can also enjoy this oasis.

The rambling building of local stone is packed full of an arres
ing mixture of antiques and Bruno's own modern art. The main si
ting-room, with its great fireplace and white couches, is flanked b
a long terrace where one can eat or just relax, listening to the bir
song of the wooded hills. In the summer there are musical and the
atrical evenings. In the rest of the house, stone and brick arche
frame decoratively painted doors and parchment-shaded lights illu
minate old coloured wooden carvings. The bedrooms will inspir
many a pleasant dream.

The atmosphere is hushed, but in a relaxed rather than reveren
manner and, birdsong aside, the only sound is of operatic aria
gently playing in the background.

Nearby Todi (7 km); Orvieto (29 km).

Loc. Asproli 7, 06059 Todi,
Perugia
Tel & fax (075) 8853385
Location country house in its
own grounds
Meals breakfast; dinner on
request
Prices LL
Rooms 6 double, 2 suite all
with shower or bath, phone,
heating
Facilities pool, garden,
terrace, sitting-room

Smoking yes
Credit AE, MC, V
Children not suitable
Disabled difficult
Pets no
Closed Jan to Feb
Languages English, French,
German
Proprietor Bruno Pagliari

Perugia

Country restaurant and guest-house, Assisi

Il Morino

Staying within the walls of Assisi has become an increasingly unrewarding experience. Parking is almost always difficult, most hotel rooms are costly, and late-night noise has irritated more than a few of our reporters. This attractive restaurant and guest-house stands just outside Assisi, at Bastia Umbra in a patch of green countryside between the city walls and the towns of the Chiascio plain. The Battistelli family's farm has been protected from encroachments of city development by the local green belt policy. Within their oasis, they have tastefully converted their traditional, stone-built farmhouse into a restaurant and guest-house which provide excellent value for travellers on a low budget.

The moderate-sized bedrooms are pleasantly furnished with reproductions of what Signora Battistelli describes as "the style of our grandparents' day". Two rooms have balcony views up to Assisi.

The restaurant is run by an extremely competent chef whose menu, though Umbrian-based, often runs further afield. Many of the ingredients – including poultry, vegetables, fruit and wine – are produced by the family *azienda*.

Nearby Assisi (2 km); Santa Maria degli Angeli (1 km).

Via Spoleto 8, Bastia Umbra,
86083 Perugia
Tel & Fax (075) 8010839
Location 2 km W of Assisi,
off SS147; ample parking
Meals breakfast, lunch,
dinner
Prices rooms L; DB&B L
Rooms 10 double, with
shower and central heating
Facilities sitting-room,
restaurant, bar; garden,
minigolf, bicycles

Credit cards MC, V
Children accepted
Disabled one ground-floor
bedroom
Pets small dogs accepted
Closed never
Languages English, French
Proprietor Rosanna Battistelli

Perugia

Town hotel, Assisi

Umbra

In a city not noted for quality small-scale hotels, the delightful family-run Umbra cannot be ignored. Tucked away down a little alley off the main square, the Umbra consists of several little houses – some of which date back to the 13thC – with a small gravelled courtyard garden shaded by a pergola. The interior is comfortable, and in parts more like a private home than a hotel: there is a bright little sitting-room with Mediterranean-style tiles and brocaded wing armchairs and a series of bedrooms, mostly quite simply furnished, but each with its own character. When we returned to reconsider the hotel for this guide, we enjoyed eating in the elegant dining-room but agreed with past reports that the food was only 'all right'. Happily, there is no shortage of nearby alternative eating places.

The Umbra offers all the peace and quiet which you might hope to find in Assisi, and nothing is too much trouble for Albert Laudenzi, whose family has run the hotel for more than 50 years. We think that it is the best middle-range accommodation Perugia can offer.

Nearby Basilica of St Francis and other main sights.

Via degli Archi 6, Assisi, 06081 Perugia
Tel (075) 812240
Fax (075 813653
Location in the middle of Assisi, off Piazza del Comune, with a small garden; nearest car park some distance away
Meals breakfast, lunch, dinner
Prices LL; suites LLL
Rooms 16 double, 5 single, 4 suites, all with bath; all rooms have phone, central heating, TV; two thirds have air-conditioning
Facilities 3 sitting-rooms, bar, dining-room
Credit cards AE, DC, MC, V
Children tolerated
Disabled access difficult
Pets not accepted
Closed mid-Nov to mid-Dec, mid-Jan to mid-Mar
Proprietor Alberto Laudenzi

Perugia

Country villa, Bovara di Trevi

Casa Giulia

[Ca]sa Giulia, parts of which go back to the 14thC, is both an excel-
[len]t base for touring Umbria's famous cities (Assisi, Perugia,
[Sp]oleto and Todi are all within easy driving distance) and a great
[pla]ce in which to relax from the rigours of cultural tourism. Con-
[ven]ient for the main Spoleto-Perugia highway, but in no way dis-
[tur]bed by traffic, the villa has a withdrawn character as though time
[sto]pped still here sometime in the 1930s. The principal sitting-
[roo]m, a long rectangular area with doors and windows opening on
[to t]he garden, is full of bric-a-brac collected by the owner's grand-
[par]ents: *objets d'art*, old toys and cameras displayed in a glass-front-
[ed] bookcase, a collection of antique walking-sticks and umbrellas.
[I]n the rest of the house a solid, bourgeois atmosphere reigns.
[Th]e breakfast-room is elegant and uncluttered, with a black-and-
[whi]te marble tiled floor (though during the summer breakfast is
[ser]ved under a pergola, just in front of the house). The bedrooms
[are] a touch spartan, perhaps because some of them are located in
[the] old servants' quarters, but this is more a question of atmos-
[ph]ere than comfort. Outside, a path leads to a new pool.
[Ne]arby Assisi (22 km); Perugia (50 km); Spoleto (12 km).

[V]ia Corciano 1, Bovara di
[T]revi, 06039 Perugia
[T]el (0742) 78257
[F]ax (0742) 381632
[L]ocation in its own grounds
[ju]st outside village of Bovara,
[n]ear Trevi; own car parking
[M]eals breakfast, snacks,
[di]nner on request
[P]rices LL; 3-day min. stay
[R]ooms 7 doubles: 5 with own
[ba]th or shower; 2 sharing one
[ba]throom; 2 mini-apartments
[fo]r 3 people (minimum stay 3
days) with kitchenettes
Facilities sitting-room,
breakfast-room, garden,
swimming-pool, meeting-
room **Smoking** permitted
Credit cards accepted
Children welcome
Disabled one suitable
room with bathroom
Pets please check first
Closed never
Languages French, some
English **Proprietor** Caterina
Alessandrini Petrucci

Perugia

Old mill, Campello sul Clitunno

Il Vecchio Molino

It is a mystery how this inn, so close to the busy Perugia-Spol
road, remains such an oasis of tranquillity. Almost the only soun
of gurgling brooks winding through the leafy gardens. As befits
old mill, all the buildings live in close harmony with the river:
drive sweeps around the mill pond to a creeper-covered build
against which big old grinding-stones rest. The gardens are a spi
land, with weeping willows dipping into streams on both si
Water even runs through some of the old working parts, where
mill machinery has been built into the decorative scheme.

There seems to be no end to the number of public rooms
furnished in a highly individual manner: elegant white couche
front of a big brick fireplace, surmounted by carved wooden lan
tables with lecterns bearing early editions of Dante's *Purgato*
mill wheels used as doors. The bedrooms were, we were relieve
note, pleasingly dry and decorated in a restrained manner v
fine antiques, the white walls lit up by parchment-shaded lamps

Remember that the hotel is popular in the wedding season
during the Spoleto festival.

Nearby Spoleto (11 km); Perugia (50 km).

Loc.Pissignano, Via del
Tempio 34, 06042 Perugia
Tel (0743) 521122
Fax (0743) 275097
Location 50 km SE of Perugia
between Trevi and Spoleto;
in its own grounds by the
Clitunno river; ample car
parking
Meals breakfast
Prices LL
Rooms 2 single, 7 double,
5 suites, all with bath or
shower, phone, minibar;
some with air-conditioning
Facilities sitting-rooms, bar,
gardens
Smoking permitted
Credit cards AE, DC, EC, M
V
Children welcome
Disabled access difficult
Pets dogs not accepted
Closed Nov-Mar
Languages English, French,
Spanish
Proprietor Rapanelli, Anna-
Maria

Perugia

Hilltop hotel, Canalicchio

Relais il Canalicchio

ne of the paradoxes of modern Italy is that what were once the
odest homes of farmers and artisans have become, with careful
storation, exemplars of modern taste and comfort. What makes
is possible is the Italian genius for combining everyday materials
quality – brick, wood, plaster, terracotta – with style and flair.

The owners of Relais Il Canalicchio have taken over most of the
mi-fortified, hilltop town of the same name and created a hotel
at not only respects the native Umbrian qualities but imaginative-
enhances them with contemporary Italian panache. Public
ooms are in the old working areas of the mill: brick arches and the
assive grinding-stones set off the comfortable, elegant furniture.
he plain plaster walls are decorated with English prints, oil por-
aits and brilliant local ceramics. An old wine-press remains.

Each bedroom has been individually furnished; some have ter-
ace gardens and many have superb views. The restaurant serves
xquisitely prepared produce from its own farm. If you feel guilty
out such hedonism, there is a gym, a pool and a sauna. Even if
u are a prince, this is one hamlet certainly good enough for you.
earby Perugia, Assisi, Gubbio, Todi (all within 40 km).

Via della Piazza 13, 06050
Canalicchio, Perugia
Tel (075) 8707325
Fax (075) 8707296
Location quiet hill-top village
40 km SE of Perugia
Meals breakfast, lunch,
dinner
Prices LL-LLLL
Rooms 18 double; 5 single;
3 suite; all with bath or
shower, TV, air-conditioning
Facilities sitting-rooms,
restaurant, billiard-room

swimming-pool, gym, sauna,
terraces, gardens
Smoking permitted
Credit cards all
Children welcome
Disabled some rooms suitable
Pets small dogs
Closed never
Languages English, French,
German
Proprietors Antonio and
Maria Rosario Setter

Perugia

Farm guest-house, Casalini

La Rosa Canina

A long and winding track takes you out of the village of Casalini fo almost 3 km before you reach the hushed, olive-flanked valle where La Rosa Canina lies. Sandro Belardinelli and his wife mad their home here in 1989, setting aside part of two 15thC cottages a guest quarters.

The dog-rose, from which the farm takes its name, is just one of the profusion of flowers which give the banks of the front garde their perennial colour. Behind the house, the menagerie of an mals and the wire-fenced vegetable garden breathe real country li ing into what might have been just another converted farmhouse.

Inside, the guest rooms are reasonably proportioned and fur nished with a hotch-potch of furniture, old and not so old. Th wooden mangers in the downstairs dining-room are a reminde that it was once a cattle stall. The dinner menu, based upon trad tional *cucina umbra*, varies according to season, but Swiss-bor Signora Belardinelli places emphasis on the quality of her food all vegetables are home produce, as is the olive oil, much of th meat, and the jam on the breakfast table.

Nearby Lake Trasimeno (8 km); Panicale (8 km).

Via dei Mandorli 23,
Loc. Casalini, Panicale, 06064
Perugia
Tel & fax (075) 8350660
E-mail larosaca@in.it
Website www.altair2000.it/rosacanina
Location 3 km along a track,
above the village of Casalini,
ample car parking.
Meals breakfast and dinner
Prices DB&B L; minimum
stay 3 nights.
Rooms 3 double rooms and
2 family rooms, 2 with

shower; all rooms centrally
heated.
Facilities restaurant; garden,
swimming-pool, riding
(lessons also available),
archery , table-tennis, bowls
Credit cards AE, EC, MC, V
Children accepted
Disabled no special facilities
Pets not accepted
Closed Nov to Easter.
Languages German, some
English **Proprietor** Sandro
Belardinelli

Perugia

Relais La Fattoria

n the hills behind Lake Trasimeno lies the small medieval town
Castel Rigone, a mere handful of houses grouped about a hand-
me piazza, and right at its centre is this pleasant, family-run hotel
cupying what was once a manor house.

You feel a sense of welcome the moment you step inside the
ception, with its wooden ceiling, stone walls and comfortable
ole sofas; keen young staff are on hand. The public rooms are
stefully decorated, with Persian rugs on the polished cork floors
d bright modern paintings on the white walls. The only addition
the building that has been allowed by the Italian Fine Arts
nistry is a restaurant perfectly in keeping with the original style.
shes include fresh fish from the lake. Bed-rooms have been
signed with an eye more to modern comfort than to individual
le and some have lake views. The bathrooms are bright and new.
Along the entire front of the house is a terrace with sitting areas
d a small swimming-pool. An extensive buffet breakfast (home-
ade bread and jams, cheeses and cured meats) is served here in
e weather.

earby Perugia (27 km); Assisi (35 km); Gubbio (50 km).

ia Rigone 1, Castel Rigone,
ago Trasimeno, 06060
erugia
el (075) 845322
ax (075) 845197
Location 27 km NW of
erugia, in centre of town; car
arking nearby
Meals breakfast, lunch, dinner
Prices L-LLL
Rooms 3 single, 23 double, 3
unior suites, all with bath or
hower (suites with Jacuzzis),
hone, TV, minibar

Facilities sitting-room,
restaurant, terrace/garden,
swimming-pool
Smoking permitted
Credit cards AE, DC, EC, MC,
V
Children welcome
Disabled no special facilities
Pets please check first
Closed never; restaurant only,
Jan
Languages English, French,
German
Proprietors Pammelati family

Perugia

Converted castle, Cenerente

Castello dell'Oscáno

At first sight Castello dell'Oscáno appears like a fairytale mediev castle: ivy-clad turrets, battlements and crenellated towers ri above a steep, hillside pine forest. In fact, this is an 18thC re-cr ation, and the inside reveals the 18thC's genius for civilized living

The interiors are finely proportioned, spacious and light. Th hall rises the entire height of the castle, with an imposing carve stairway, polished wood floors and neo-Gothic windows. One pu lic room leads into another, all filled with the castle's original fu niture: a library which will entrance any bibliophile with its carve Classical book-cases and 18thC volumes; sitting-rooms with woode panelling, tapestries and sculpted fireplaces; a dining-room wit old display cases full of Deruta pottery.

Upstairs, the floors are of geometrically patterned, black-an white marble. There are only ten bedrooms in the castle, each wit its own antique furnishing. The remainder, in the Villa Ada ne door, are less exciting and cheaper. The most spectacular (b strictly for the agile) is in the turret, with a four-poster bed and door to the ramparts which look over the romantic gardens belov
Nearby Perugia (5 km); Assisi (28 km); Gubbio (40 km).

Loc. Cenerente, 06134
Perugia
Tel (075) 690 125
Fax (075) 690 666
Location on a hillside in its
own grounds; ample car
parking
Meals breakfast, dinner
Prices LLLL (Castello)– LL
(Villa Ada)
Rooms 11 double (Castello),
8 double, 2 single (Villa Ada);
all with bath or shower,
phone, TV, minibar, air-
conditioning
Facilities bar, gardens,
swimming-pool (shared with
bed-and-breakfast)
Smoking permitted
Credit cards AE, DC, EC, MC,
V
Children welcome
Disabled 1 suitable bedroom
Pets accepted
Closed never; restaurant
only, 15 Jan to 15 Feb
Languages English, French
Manager Maurizio Bussolati

Perugia

Town villa, Foligno

Villa Roncalli

n't be put off by the depressing light-industrial surroundings in
ich this splendid 18thC villa now finds itself. The tall chestnut
es which line the drive and encircle this former hunting lodge
een off the outside world almost entirely.

Although the present owners acquired the villa only relatively
cently, they have succeeded in creating within it the atmosphere
a family home. The public rooms are furnished with magnificent
ces of antique furniture and paintings.

The ground floor is dominated by the elegant dining-room, for-
rly the villa's entrance hall, with its long sideboard and massive
ss-fronted wine cabinet. Angelo's wife Alessandra runs the
chen, which has become one of the gastronomic temples of cen-
l Umbria, while their daughter Maria Luisa oversees the front-of-
use with amiable efficiency.

Upstairs, on the *piano nobile*, four airy bedrooms with large shut-
ed windows lead off the cool, frescoed sitting-room, while the
nainder are in the mansarded second floor. Each is furnished
ulently in a timeless modern style.

arby Spello (7 km); Montefalco (12 km); Assisi (15 km).

ia Roma 25, Foligno, 06034
erugia
el (0742) 391091
ax (0742) 391001
ocation 1.5 km S of Foligno;
mple parking
Meals breakfast, lunch,
dinner
Prices rooms L-LL; DB&B
LL
Rooms 8 double, 2 singles
ith shower, air-conditioning,
elevision, minibar, heating

Facilities sitting-room,
breakfast room, restaurant,
bar
Credit cards DC, AE, V, MC
Children accepted
Disabled no facilities
Pets not accepted
Closed never
Languages English, French
Proprietors Angelo and
Alessandra Scolastra

Perugia

Villa Montegranelli

The fact that this 18thC villa is based on an original fortified building of the 13thC helps to explain the unadorned severity of the
exterior. Massive and square, built of hewn stone, it stands in its
own park surrounded by pines and centuries-old cypresses. From
the gardens there is a view over to the light-grey stone city hanging
on to the mountainside (a view that unfortunately includes the
cement factory that has been allowed next to this dignified town).

In stark contrast, most of the interiors are in a light 18thC style,
airily spacious public rooms with ornate plasterwork, frescoes and
elaborate marble door surrounds, probably more suitable for the
numerous weddings and official functions that take place here
than for sitting and relaxing. The bedrooms are much more simply
done (except for the main suite) and some are quite small. They
all have excellent bathrooms.

The breakfast- and dining-rooms are in the lower, 13thC, part of
the villa, with thick stone walls, vaulted ceilings and old brick arches. It is renowned for its restaurant, and you will appreciate the
sophisticated cuisine and attentive service.

Nearby Gubbio (5 km); Perugia (38 km); Assisi (35 km).

Loc. Monteluiano, Gubbio,
06024 Perugia
Tel (075) 9220185
Fax (075) 9273372
Location 5 km SW of Gubbio,
in its own grounds; ample car
parking
Meals breakfast,lunch, dinner
Prices LL-LLL
Rooms 20 double, 1 single,
all with bath or shower,
phone, TV, minibar
Facilities sitting-rooms,

restaurant, gardens
Smoking permitted except in
restaurant
Credit cards AE, DC, EC, MC,
V
Children welcome
Disabled no special facilities
Pets dogs accepted
Closed never
Languages English, French
Proprietor Salvatore Mongelli

Perugia

Farm guest-house, Montecastello Vibio

Fattoria di Vibio

Occasionally, the whole atmosphere of a place is captured by a small detail: here it is the hand-painted pottery used to serve Signora Saladini's delicious meals which reveals the relaxed elegance of this renovated 18thC farmhouse. The style is modern rustic Italian, with pleasing open spaces, defined by white walls that contrast with the colourful fabrics and ceramics. Light, airy and well-proportioned, there is an air of effortless simplicity which, you quickly realize, required a great deal of taste and effort. Most of the bedrooms, of similar style, are in the house next door.

The Saladini family are serious about their visitors' comforts and well-being, starting in the kitchen. Much of what goes into the guests comes out of the farm or the market garden and the preparation is a spectacle in itself, open to all. The mandatory half-board should not prove a penance. If you need to lose calories, you can swim, play table-tennis, ride or walk in the magnificent countryside around; tennis is also available nearby. Or you may prefer to relax in the quiet of the garden. Otherwise, there is not much to do – but then that is the whole point of this soothing guest-house.

Nearby Todi (20 km); Orvieto (30 km).

Loc. Buchella 1a, 9-Doglio, Montescastello Vibio, 05010 Perugia
Tel (075) 8749607
Fax (075) 8780014
Location Quiet hillside farmhouse, off S448 road between Todi and Orvieto; ample car parking
Meals breakfast, lunch, dinner
Prices L-LL (half-board); one week minimum stay in August
Rooms 10 double, all with bath or shower; some with TV

Facilities sitting-room, dining-room and terrace, garden, swimming-pool, bikes, horse-riding, fishing
Smoking permitted
Credit cards AE, EC, DC, MC, V **Children** welcome
Disabled one suitable room
Pets small dogs
Closed Jan and Feb
Languages French, little English
Proprietors Gabriella, Giuseppe & Filippo Saladini

Perugia

Villa hotel, Montefalco

Villa Pambuffetti

Like Hemingway in Spain, the poet D'Annunzio seems to have stayed everywhere in Italy; however, in the case of Villa Pambuffetti the claim is better justified than most. Not only did he dedicate a poem to the nearby walled town of Montefalco (known as 'Umbria's balcony' for its unrivalled views of the region, but the villa itself has a turn-of-the-century elegance that fits the poet's legend.

Ten thousand square metres of shady garden surround the main building. Inside, furniture and decoration have been kept almost as they were at the start of the 1900s when the Pambuffetti family began taking 'paying guests': floors and panelling of seasoned oak, bamboo armchairs (which took D'Annunzio's fancy), Tiffany lamp shades and old family photographs in art nouveau frames pay tribute to a century that started optimistically. Many of the bedrooms are furnished with the family's older and finer antiques and all have bathrooms which, though recent, are, stylistically, nearly perfect. If you like a room with a view, try the tower, which has one of the six-windowed, all-round variety. The dining-room's view is more modest, but then the food deserves attention, too.
Nearby Montefalco, Assisi (30 km); Perugia (46 km).

Via della Vittoria 20,
Montefalco 06036 Perugia
Tel (0742) 379417, 378823
Fax (0742) 379245
Location just outside
Montefalco, in its own
grounds; ample car parking
Meals breakfast, dinner
Rooms 10 double; 2 single;
3 suites; 2 with bath, the rest
with shower, TV, minibar, air-
conditioning
Prices LL-LLL
Facilities sitting-room, bar

restaurant, loggia, garden,
swimming-pool
Smoking permitted
Credit cards AE, DC, MC, V
Children welcome
Disabled 2 rooms on ground
floor
Pets not accepted
Closed never
Languages English, French,
German, Spanish
Managers Alessandra and
Mauro Angelucci

Perugia

Town hotel, Panicale

Le Grotte di Boldrino

The former Palazzo Belleschi-Grifoni, hewn into the walls of the medieval brick-built hill town of Panicale, was converted only in 1990 to its present use. In contrast to its stern front, the interior is small and intimate, designed in the finest contemporary manner, with particularly imaginative use of iron and wood.

The hotel can be entered through a doorway from one of the narrow passageways of the old *borgo* or, more conveniently, via the lower restaurant entrance on the road which encircles the town. A warren-like corridor takes you to the parquet-floored bedrooms. In surprising contrast to their modern finish, they are furnished with imperious late-19thC furniture – towering walnut bedheads, and so on. Noteworthy also is the gentle use of lighting.

The reputation of the downstairs restaurant is increasing by leaps and bounds. Again, you find a pleasing juxtaposition of old and new, with the unplastered medieval wall and traditional oak and brick-tile ceiling against the modern plastered walls and iron railings of the restaurant's upper gallery. The short, mainly Umbrian, menu offers a variety of local specialities.

Nearby Castiglione del Lago (15 km); Città della Pieve (25 km).

Via Virgilio Cappari 30,
Panicale, 06064 Perugia
Tel (075) 837161
Fax (075) 837166
Location built into the town walls, parking nearby
Meals breakfast, lunch and dinner
Prices rooms L; restaurant LL
Rooms 9 double rooms, 2 singles, all with bath or shower, TV, telephone
Facilities restaurant, breakfast room, sitting-room
Credit cards AE, DC, V
Children accepted
Disabled access difficult
Pets small pets accepted
Closed never
Languages French, some English
Proprietor Attilio Spadoni

Perugia

Country villa hotel, Panicale

Villa di Montesolare

High walls keep out the arid scenery around, enclosing the stuccoed villa in a green oasis. The present building dates back to 178￼ although the 16thC chapel in the garden suggests a much earlie￼ house was on the site. When the present owners bought it, they s￼ about restoring the 19thC garden (and the secret garden behin￼ it), building the swimming-pool a discreet distance away, and co￼ verting the villa without interfering with its patrician character.

The result is one of the most comfortable country retreats of th￼ Trasimeno area. The bedrooms of the villa retain their origina￼ character – beamed ceilings, quarry tile floors and whitewashe￼ walls, furnished in squirely fashion with turn-of-the-century hig￼ backed beds, cabinets and wardrobes. The cool blue sitting-roo￼ on the *piano nobile* certainly is noble, while the dining-rooms an￼ the bar downstairs have been housed in the villa's wine *cantina*.

In 1995, Mrs Strunk and her husband Filippo completed th￼ conversion of a *casa colonica* which stands outside the walls. The￼ divided it into five suites, building by it the villa's second swim￼ ming-pool. Here the rooms are simply furnished in country style.
Nearby Panicale (12 km); Città della Pieve (25 km).

Loc. Colle San Paolo,
Panicale, 06070 Perugia
Tel (075) 832376
Fax (075) 8355462
Location 2 km N of the SS
220, direction Colle S. Paolo;
ample car parking
Meals breakfast, lunch and
dinner
Prices DB&B LL-LLL;
minimum stay three days
Rooms 8 double rooms with
bathroom and two suites in

the villa; 5 suites in annex
Facilities two dining-rooms,
bar, sitting-room; two
swimming-pools, clay tennis
court, bowls, riding
Credit cards DC, MC, V
Children accepted
Disabled no special facilities
Pets if small, well-behaved
Closed never
Languages English, German,
French
Proprietor Rosemarie Strunk

Perugia

Country villa guest-house, Ponte Pattoli

Il Covone

Parts of Villa Il Covone date back to medieval times – the tower was once used to watch over the nearby Tiber. Today, the visitor is more conscious of the 18thC additions and the romantically peeling 19thC façade, which gives it the air of a classic Italianate villa.

The main hall, once an open courtyard, now glassed over, and the downstairs sitting-rooms hold the family accretions of several centuries – portraits hanging higgledy-piggledy on cracking plaster remind you that this is still the Taticchi family's home. Upstairs, the guest quarters comprise bedrooms of different shapes and sizes, each spacious and high-ceilinged. The furniture has certainly seen better days (as has the house), but that is exactly what gives the place its charm. The eight rooms in the annex, across the way in the equestrian centre, are more modern, and perhaps more comfortable, but lack the fading splendour of the main house.

Dinner, shared with the family around one large table, includes Umbrian specialities such as *gnocchetti di ricotta* (small potato dumplings in a ricotta cheese sauce), pork roasted in the wood oven and *gelato in cialda* (ice cream in a nest of sponge).

Nearby Perugia (10 km); Assisi (30 km).

Strada della Fratticiola 2,
Ponte Pattoli, 06080 Perugia
Tel (075) 694140
Fax (075) 694503
Location 2 km W of SS3-bis;
gardens and private car
parking
Meals breakfast, lunch and
evening meal
Prices rooms L; DB&B LL
Rooms 4 double rooms in
villa, not all with private
bathroom; 8 double rooms
with shower, in annex

Facilities sitting room,
dining-room; garden, horse-
riding (lessons available)
Credit cards MC, V
Children accepted
Disabled no facilities
available
Pets small pets only
Closed never
Languages Some English
Proprietors Cesare and Elena
Taticchi

Perugia

Semi di Mela

A difficult track takes you down, past the castle of Petroia, to th
restored *casa colonica*, a farm worker's cottage over a decade ago.
downstairs beam shows that it was already standing in 1690, but i
recent restoration has rather deprived it of that rough, rural cha
acter. The traditional oak and brick ceilings remain, but th
smooth plasterwork and neat carpentry are all too perfect.

The bedrooms are comfortable, furnished simply in tradition
rustic style. Every window opens on to awesome views of th
Appennine mountains to the east of Gubbio.

Francesco Pellegrini grows organic food for the supper table o
his ten acres of land, as well as olives and cereal crops, whil
Antonella tends the poultry which roam freely around the yar
and runs the kitchen. The emphasis of the evenings is that ver
Italian pursuit of *stare insieme* (getting together). Individual tabl
in the dining-room have recently been replaced with a single larg
one at which Antonella and Francesco eat with their guests. The
limited knowledge of English or other languages is made up for b
the warmth of their hospitality.

Nearby Gubbio (15 km); Perugia (25 km).

Loc. Petroia 36, Scritto,
Gubbio, 06020 Perugia
Tel & fax (075) 920039
Location 2 km E of the SS298
between Perugia and Gubbio
Meals breakfast and dinner
Prices DB&B L; minimum
stay two days, one week in
August
Rooms 5 double rooms (1 for
four people) with shower
Facilities sitting/dining-
room; terrace, garden,

archery, bowls
Credit cards not accepted
Children accepted
Disabled no special facilities
Pets not accepted
Closed 6 Jan to early Mar
Languages some English
Proprietors Antonella
Requale & Francesco
Pellegrini

Perugia

Town hotel, Spoleto

Gattapone

There are two things you can do in this hotel just outside Spoleto's centre. The most obvious is to gape at the unparalleled views of the 13thC Bridge of Towers spanning the Tessino Valley. The other is to enjoy the quaintness of its Sixties jet-set decoration, all wood, glass, chrome and leather. If you tire, as some do, of the rustic antique look, then you will enjoy the now dated, but meticulously maintained 'modern' style.

The hotel is a favourite of the Festival crowd, and the walls of the bar are festooned with pictures of the famous and would-be famous who throng its *salons* late into the evening. Even if you do not stay at the Gattapone, you will notice it. From the outside it looks like a solid, two-storey villa with classic ochre walls and green shutters. Inside, one notices how the original building and its more modern extension have been constructed downwards to exploit the hillside position. Many of the bedrooms have small terraces and large picture windows to capture the panorama.

We visited the hotel in low season and enjoyed the peace and quiet. During the Festival (June-July), rooms are hard to get.

Nearby Assisi 48 km; Todi 42 km; Perugia 63 km.

Via del Ponte 6, Spoleto,
06049 Perugia
Tel (0743) 223447
Fax (0743) 223448
Location on hillside, just
outside historic centre of
Spoleto; no special parking
facilities
Meals breakfast
Prices LL-LLL
Rooms 7 double, 7 junior
suites, all with bath or
shower, phone,

TV, minibar
Facilities breakfast-room,
sitting-room, bar, terrace
Smoking permitted
Credit cards AE, DC, EC, MC,
V
Children welcome
Disabled no special facilities
Pets accepted
Closed never
Languages English, French
Proprietor Pier Giulio Hanke

Perugia

Country hotel, Spoleto

La Macchia

Spoleto, one of the most interesting of the southern Umbrian towns, is also one of the most congested, with a confusing one-way system and few places to park. From late June until mid-July, during Spoleto's world-famous Festival of Two Worlds, it is also notoriously difficult to find a room. This quiet hotel, tucked away in the fold of a hillside, yet close to the centre, offers a welcome alternative for those in search of a peaceful stay.

Carla and Claudio's hotel started life in the 1980s as a country *osteria* specializing in the local *cucina spoletana*. It was only recently that they opened their hotel. A separate entrance spares guests from the occasional inconvenience caused by large dinners in the downstairs banqueting room. The style throughout is modern, though the old barn, now a shady portico, and the gnarled olive tree in the front courtyard, are a reminder of the building's original use.

In each of the well-lit bedrooms, the chestnut furniture has been made by local craftsmen. Some beds have old wrought-iron heads and splendidly firm bases.

Nearby Spoleto (2 km); Fonti di Clitunno (10 km).

Loc. Licina 11, Spoleto 06049 Perugia
Tel & fax (0743) 49059
Location 0.5 km from the old via Flaminia, just N of Spoleto; ample car parking
Meals breakfast, lunch, dinner
Prices rooms L with breakfast
Rooms 10 double, 1 single with shower, air-conditioning, satellite television, minibar, central heating

Facilities sitting-room, breakfast room, bar, restaurant, garden
Credit cards AE, DC, MC, V
Children accepted
Disabled 2 bedrooms
Pets not accepted
Closed never; restaurant only, Tue
Languages English
Proprietors Carla Marini and Claudio Sabatini

Perugia

San Luca

When Pope Innocent II came to this spot in 1198, his holy presence is reputed to have caused a fountain miraculously to begin spouting clear and plentiful water, thus giving immediate relief and renewed strength to himself and his retinue. Today the site is occupied by an impressive 19thC building with soft yellow painted walls, wooden doors and shutters, and a red-tiled roof, which was transformed after extensive renovation into an elegant hotel in 1995. The yellow colour scheme continues inside in the light, sunny hallway and sitting areas, where comfortable armchairs, some upholstered in bright yellow, others, more modern, in black leather, blend stylishly with antique furniture, a display of china screens and attractive arrangements of flowers and plants. Several of the pastel-toned bedrooms have a balcony or terrace; all of them are soundproofed and have large bathrooms with telephones.

Right in the centre of Spoleto, but peacefully set in lush gardens, the San Luca also has a roof garden as well as a spacious internal courtyard, where it is still possible to sample the 'therapeutic' properties of the waters. New to the guide; we would welcome reports.

Nearby Assisi 48 km; Todi 42 km.

Via Interna delle Mura 21,
Spoleto 06049, Perugia
Tel (0743) 223399
Fax (0743) 223800
Location in historic city centre; car parking
Meals buffet breakfast
Prices LL
Rooms 32 double, 2 single, 1 suite, all with bath (some with Jacuzzi), 5 with shower, phone, air-conditioning, minibar, hairdrier, safe

Facilities 2 sitting-rooms, breakfast-room, conference room, 2 lifts, courtyard, garden, roof garden
Smoking allowed
Credit cards AE, MC, DC, V
Children welcome
Disabled two adapted rooms
Pets smalll dogs accepted
Closed never
Languages English, German, French
Proprietor Daniela Zuccari

Perugia

San Valentino

When we last inspected San Valentino, we sensed that a slightly quirky atmosphere reigned in this former monastery, as if the buildings themselves had not fully accepted their conversion to the needs of a luxury hotel. At least, this was our impression sitting in the former church which served as the social hub of the complex.

Still in place was a lovely 13thC Umbrian fresco of the Crucifixion, but where the altar might have been was a bar and below, in the crypt, there was a piano to encourage late night crooners to join in with *My Way* rather than *Dies Irae.* We were worried that some of the guests looked a little glum, as if caught in the act of sacrilege. The remainder of the hotel, more conventional in decoration and atmosphere, fully exploited its prime position looking over to the gracious silhouette of nearby Todi.

San Valentino has a new proprietor and we understand that it has again undergone a major renovation programme. Reports welcome.

Nearby Todi (4 km); Perugia (35 km); Orvieto (35 km).

Loc. San Valentino, Todi, 06059 Perugia
Tel (075) 8944103,
Meals breakfast, snacks
Location in its own grounds, on hillside outside Todi; ample car parking
Prices LL-LLL-LLLL
Rooms 4 double, 1 single, 3 suites, all with bath or shower
Facilities breakfast-room, sitting-room, bar, garden, swimming-pool, tennis
Smoking permitted
Credit cards AE, MC, DC, V
Children please check first
Disabled not suitable
Pets small dogs accepted
Closed variable
Languages French, Spanish, some English
Proprietor Sig. Baresi

Perugia

Town hotel, Torgiano

Le Tre Vaselle

Three monastic wine jugs discovered during the restoration of the original 17thC *palazzo* are what give this exceptional hotel its name and its theme: wine. Owned by the Lungarotti family, makers of Umbria's finest vintages, the *palazzo* is packed with still lifes of grapes, prints of the gods carousing and statues of Bacchus. However, nothing but sober professionalism characterizes the day-to-day management.

Bedrooms, some in a more modern building behind the main one and others in a luxury annexe a short walk away, are all furnished to the highest standards: comfortable striped sofas, antique chests, individually chosen prints and lamps give an air of unrushed elegance. Public rooms are open and spacious, spanned by sweeping white arches and softly lit. Breakfast, an extensive buffet, is served on a secluded back terrace. The restaurant is outstanding, with a wine-list the size of a telephone directory.

A recent visitor to Le Tre Vaselle could report only improvements. It could not be more professional; you could not feel more at home.

Nearby Deruta (5 km); Perugia (8 km); Assisi (16 km).

Via Garibaldi 48, Torgiano, 06089 Perugia
Tel (075) 9880447
Fax (075) 9880214
Location in quiet street of village of Torgiano, 13 km SE of Perugia; car parking in nearby piazza
Meals breakfast, lunch, dinner
Prices LL-LLLL
Rooms 52 double, 2 singles, 7 suites; most with bath, some with shower; all rooms have central heating, air-conditioning, phone, TV
Facilities sitting-rooms, dining-rooms, breakfast-room, bar, terrace, swimming- pool, sauna
Smoking permitted
Credit cards AE, DC, MC, V
Children welcome
Disabled access possible
Pets not accepted
Closed never
Languages English, French, German
Manager Giovanni Margheritini

Terni

Pomurlo Vecchio/Le Casette

Lazzaro Minghelli's 350-acre farm estate stretches from the south ern shores of Lago di Corbara almost as far as Baschi. His romantic family home, Pomurlo Vecchio, is an eccentric 12thC tower, jutting out of a wooded hillock. It also has four small apartments, each with its separate entrance. They are homely, though rather frayed at the edges and in need of redecoration.

The principal guest accommodation, however, Le Casette stands on the other side of the estate, towards Baschi. Its three stone cottages have been recently rebuilt around a central swim ming-pool on a hillside ridge. Though lacking the patina of age they provide a summer oasis which is particularly suitable for fami lies, Each room is simply decorated, with white plaster and expose stone walls and comfortably furnished.

The restaurant, overseen by daughter Daniela, is noteworthy Each course has a genuine farmhouse taste — 80 per cent of th ingredients are organically grown on the estate. This is comple mented by the charm and warmth of the family, who eat with the guests and do everything to make them feel at home.

Nearby Orvieto (15 km); Todi (20 km).

Loc. Pomurlo Vecchio, Baschi, 05023 Terni
Tel (0744) 950190/950475
Fax (0744) 950500
Location 1 km S of SS448 near Lago di Corbara; or 5 km E of Baschi towards Montecchio
Meals lunch, dinner
Prices rooms L; DB&B L-LL; minimum stay one week in August
Rooms 3 small apartments in main villa; 8 double rooms, 6 apartments in Le Casette complex (about 1 mile away); all with shower, refrigerator and breakfast
Facilities central heating; restaurant, bar; swimming-pool, horse-riding **Credit cards** none **Children** welcome
Disabled 3 bedrooms
Pets by prior arrangement
Closed never
Languages some English
Proprietor Lazzaro and Daniela Minghelli

Terni

Country hotel, Baschi

Villa Bellago

Undeniably modern, but stylish in its own way, Villa Bellago will
appeal to travellers who enjoy contemporary comforts and the
full range of facilities. Magnificently situated on the shores of
Lago di Corbara, a man-made lake, the 'villa' was originally a set
of 19thC farm buildings, but is now rigorously updated. The
low-slung buildings, pleasantly rose-tinted, fit well into the tree-
filled, undulating grounds that lead down to the lake. The
interiors are defined by clean lines, occasionally broken by a
traditional brick arch or fire-place. Furnishings are stylishly
contemporary, and a minimalist approach to decoration gives a
spacious feel.

The hotel certainly makes full use of its lakeside location: large
picture windows carry your eyes over its rippling surface to the sloping green hills beyond. The gardens are meticulously cared for,
with acres of rolling lawns and brightly coloured flowers in
squat terracotta urns, and there is an outdoor pergola next to the
restaurant where you can enjoy not just your meal and the view but
also a cool evening breeze from the lake.

Nearby Orvieto (10 km); Todi (15 km).

Baschi, Strada per Todi (SS
448) 05023 Terni
Tel (0744) 950521
Fax (0744) 950524
Location lakeside location
on SS 448 between Orvieto
and Todi; own grounds,
ample car parking
Meals breakfast, lunch,
dinner
Prices L-LL
Rooms 10 double, 2 suites, all
with bath or shower, phone,
TV, minibar

Facilities sitting-room, bar,
restaurant, garden, tennis
court, swimming-pool, bil-
liards, five-a-side football,
gym, sauna
Smoking permitted
Credit cards AE, DC, EC, MC,
V **Children** welcome
Disabled 2 adapted rooms
Pets check first **Closed** never;
restaurant only, Tue
Languages English, French
Manager Massimiliano
Benedetti

Terni

Dei Priori

Tucked away in a quiet alley in the medieval heart of one of south ern Umbria's unsung towns, this friendly small hotel provides a ideal staging post for travellers who prefer the 'backroads' rou along the via Flaminia to Rome. As well as the magnificent Piazz dei Priori, the town's Romanesque *duomo* and the 14thC Palazz del Podestà provide ample reason for an overnight detour.

The meat hooks in the bricked, vaulted ceiling of the entranc hall indicate that it was once the food store for the *palazz* Upstairs, the sitting-rooms on the *piano nobile*, with their carve stone architraves, are altogether more worthy.

A lift, or a grandiose black oval staircase, takes you up to th comfortable modern bedrooms which look out into the centr courtyard or over the pantiled roofs of the medieval *borgo*. A fe have their own small balconies.

Downstairs, the restaurant spills out into the courtyard in th summer months. Its menu is mainly Umbrian (the local pasta dis is *manfricoli*), although the Venetian chef adds the occasion northern dish.

Nearby Ponte di Augusto (2 km); Otricoli (14 km).

Vicolo del Comune 4,
Narni, 05035 Terni
Tel & fax (0744) 726843
Location 20 m from the
town's main Piazza dei Priori
Meals Breakfast, lunch,
dinner
Prices rooms L
Rooms 11 double, 5 single,
1 suite, all with shower,
television, radio, minibar,
central heating; 7 rooms with
air-conditioning

Facilities sitting-room,
breakfast room, bar,
restaurant with tables also in
the interior courtyard
Credit cards AE, DC, MC, V
Children accepted
Disabled no facilities
Pets small well-behaved
animals accepted
Closed never
Languages some English
Proprietor Maurizio Bravi

Terni

La Badia

Arriving at twilight at La Badia is like landing in a scene from a Gothic novel: ruined arches, rooks cawing from a crenellated bell-tower, dark cypresses silhouetted against the sky and, across the valley, the evening profile of Orvieto's cathedral, secure on its fortress crag. But the golden stone monastery on the hill, surrounded by Umbria's intense green countryside, soon reveals itself as an outstanding hotel that would have delighted any Renaissance cardinal.

Restraint is the hallmark of this fine building's conversion into a distinctive hotel. The robust architecture of the old abbey is always allowed to speak for itself, and modern embellishments have been kept to a minimum. The heavy wooden period furniture goes well with the massive stone walls; wrought-iron lights illuminate vaulted ceilings; floors are either of plain or geometrically patterned terracotta. Here and there, an unexpectedly-placed church pew reminds the guest of what once was.

On the hill behind, is a pool fit for a pope. In front of the abbey, beside the famous 12-sided tower, is a peaceful garden where the meditative visitor can contemplate the view of Orvieto.

Nearby Orvieto (5 km); Todi (40 km); Viterbo (45 km).

Loc. La Badia, Orvieto, 05019 Terni	**Facilities** sitting-room, breakfast-room, bar, restaurant, conference-room, tennis-court, swimming-pool
Tel (07633) 01959	
Fax (07633) 05396	
Location on quiet hillside, 5 km S of Orvieto	**Smoking** permitted
Meals breakfast, lunch, dinner	**Credit cards** AE, V
Prices LL-LLLL	**Children** welcome
Rooms 3 single, 16 double, 7 suites; all with bath or shower; all rooms have phone, air-conditioning, central heating	**Disabled** access difficult
	Pets not allowed
	Closed Jan and Feb
	Languages English
	Proprietor Luisa Fiume

Terni

Country villa, Orvieto (Canale)

Fattoria La Cacciata

It is a short drive up from the small village of Canale, through row
of vineyards, to Villa La Cacciata. Across the valley stands Orvieto
cathedral, seated majestically on its limestone pedestal; the villa'
swimming-pool must surely have one of the top ten locations in a
of Italy.

The main building, an aristocratic villa with a 19thC facelif
remains the home of *avvocato* Belcapo and his family, while fou
stone farm buildings around it have been converted into simpl
guest accommodation. Each bedroom retains the atmosphere of
farm cottage: beamed and tiled ceilings and terracotta floors wit
simple, somewhat spartan, furnishings. Most of them have idylli
pastoral views out over the estate. Bathrooms are shared, but this
more than reflected in the low charges.

The Belcapo family's estate produces one of the area's premie
Orvieto Classico wines and fine olive oil.

The kitchen and restaurant in one of the buildings are period
cally used for cookery courses. For the remainder of the time, th
family offer a tempting menu of strictly Umbrian fare.

Nearby Orvieto's cathedral and Pozzo di San Patrizio (4 km).

Loc. La Cacciata 6, Orvieto,
05010 Terni
Tel (0763) 300892-305481
Fax (0763) 341373
Location Near the village of
Canale, S of Orvieto
Meals breakfast, dinner on
request
Prices rooms L; DB&B L
Rooms 11 double rooms,
sharing 10 bathrooms,
central heating
Facilities sitting-room with
television in each building,
restaurant, bar; swimming-
pool, garden, riding
Credit cards none
Children accepted
Disabled no facilities
Pets not accepted
Closed Christmas period
Languages some English
Proprietor Settimio Belcapo

Terni

Country villa, Orvieto

Villa Ciconia

otected from the nearby busy road and the encroachments of
rvieto's new suburbs by its tree-filled gardens, La Ciconia is a
nall, attractive 16thC grey stone villa with two bays of windows
anking an arched entrance. Inside, one encounters a variety of
yles, from the spacious ground-floor public rooms with geomet-
c, polychrome tiled floors, massive stone fireplaces and frescoed
iezes to the simpler but more restful sitting-rooms on the upper
oor, where leather couches add a zestful note of modernity.

The bedrooms are in a more rustic style, with wrought-iron or
ur-poster beds and antique chests that combine well with the
posed roof-beams and warm, terracotta floors. Bathrooms are
anking new and most have a shower rather than a bath.

The gardens are a delight, bounded by two streams. There is,
fortunately, some noise from the road outside. The restaurant
rves Umbrian specialities with oil and wine from the owner's
rms - popular for weddings, so it may get busy at weekends.

A pleasant alternative to La Badia (page 141) if the latter is full
you find it too expensive.

earby Orvieto (3 km); Todi (33 km); Perugia (78 km).

Loc. Ciconia, Via dei Tigli 69, Orvieto, 05018 Terni	(L20,000 per day) **Facilities** sitting-rooms, dining-room, breakfast-room, garden
Tel (0763) 305582/3	
Fax (0763) 302077	
Location just outside Orvieto n its own grounds, ample car parking	**Smoking** allowed **Credit cards** AE, DC, EC, MC, V **Children** welcome
Meals breakfast, lunch, dinner	**Disabled** not suitable **Pets** please check first
Prices LL-LLL	**Closed** mid-Jan to mid-Feb; restaurant only, Mon
Rooms 9 double, 1 single, all with bath (one with acuzzi), phone, satellite TV, ninibar, air-conditioning	**Languages** English **Proprietor** Valentino Petrangeli

Terni

Fattoria di Titignano

Fatttoria di Titignano is not a place for people in search of refine
luxury. It is a simple, honest, rural guest-house whose attraction
are not those of a professionally run, starred hotel but of a workin
farm estate that gives a warm welcome.

Owned by the aristocratic Corsini family and set in two thousan
hectares, the hamlet stands on a hillside overlooking the Tibe
Valley and Lake Corbara. On one side of the wide street (when w
visited, it was being paved with cobble-stones at the expense of th
European Community) is the principal house containing the pub
lic rooms and some of the bedrooms. A lovely loggia on the fir
floor, overlooks the church and the former farm workers' cottage
where there are more bedrooms and a few small apartments.

The general style is battered rustic with hints of former elegance
carved stone doors and fireplaces, gloomy oil paintings and hig
wooden ceilings. Bedrooms vary in size and decoration: in th
farmers' cottages, they are smaller and more modern, and th
excellent bathrooms have been newly installed. Make a point o
visiting the wine cellars and the cheese dairy.

Nearby Orvieto (25 km); Todi (23 km).

Loc. Titignano, Orvieto,
05010 Terni
Tel (0763) 308022
Fax (0763) 308002
Location 25 km NE of
Orvieto, off the SS 79 bis
Meals breakfast, dinner
Prices L
Rooms 6 double, all with
bath or shower; 5 apartments
Facilities sitting-room, dining-
room, terrace, swimming-
pool

Smoking allowed
Credit cards not accepted
Children welcome; 30%
discount for 3rd bed in room
Disabled not suitable
Pets accepted
Closed never
Languages English, French
Managers Giulio and Monica
Fontani

Arezzo

Borgo Antico

useful address in a part of Tuscany not over-supplied with
commendable hotels in spite of the great countryside.
edrooms are comfortable and modern. Public areas retain
ore of the character of the original palazzo. Golf, swim-
ing, tennis, riding and a national park nearby.

a Bernardo Dovizi 18, Bibbiena, 52011 Arezzo **Tel** (0575)
36445/46 **Fax** (0575) 536447 **Meals** breakfast, lunch, dinner
rices L **Rooms** 10 double, 2 single; all with shower, phone, TV,
inibar **Credit cards** AE, V **Children** welcome **Closed** never
anguages English

Villa Elisio

peaceful old villa in the countryside a few miles west
f Lake Trasimento which puts to good effect the familiar
ormula of white walls, tiled floors, dark beams and mellow
ooden furniture – as does the associated restaurant, Le
apezzine. Tennis and a swimming-pool. New to the guide:
e would welcome reports.

apezzine, 52040 Centoia Arezzo **Tel** (0575) 613145
ax (0575) 613167 **Meals** breakfast, lunch, dinner **Prices** LL-LLL
reakfast L15,000 DB&B LL **Rooms** 11; all with bath or shower,
V, minibar **Credit cards** AE, DC, MC, V **Children** welcome
losed never **Languages** English

Italia

cheaper alternative in Cortona to the San Michele. It
oes not have the same style, but it is very centrally located
ist a few steps from the main piazza. Furniture is a mixture
f old and new and some of the bedrooms have stylish rus-
ic antiques. Attractive rooftop terrace with views over the
aldichiana, and new restaurant, Taverna Il Ghibellina.

ia Ghibellina 5-7, Cortona, 52044 Arezzo **Tel** (0575) 630254
ax (0575) 630564 **Meals** breakfast **Prices** L **Rooms** 26 rooms,
6 with bath or shower; all with phone, TV **Credit cards** EC, MC,
Children welcome (family rooms available) **Closed** mid-Nov to
Jan **Languages** little English spoken

Restaurant with rooms, Cortona

Locanda del Molino

Converted mill built of old stone situated between a stream and a road. Fortunately, most of the bedrooms look on to the quieter side and have comfortable furniture. Downstairs is a pleasant sitting-room for guests and a restaurant serving Tuscan and Umbrian specialities, decorated with old terracotta pots and dried flowers. Swimming-pool.

Loc. Montanare, Cortona, 52044 Arezzo **Tel** (0575) 614192 **Fax** (0575) 614054 **Meals** breakfast, lunch, dinner **Prices** LL **Rooms** 8 double, all with bath or shower **Credit cards** MC, V **Children** welcome **Closed** Nov to Easter **Languages** English

Country guest-house, Terontola di Cortona

Residenza Sant'Andrea al Farinaio

We get the impression that Patrizia Nappi, owner of this delightfully maintained 13thC priest's house, does not want to be in too many guides. The regulars return year after year to enjoy this haven of civilized living surrounded by Patrizia's antiques and modern art. A place to stay for some days and completely unwind.

Loc. Sant'Andrea al Farinaio 118, Terontola di Cortona, 52040 Arezzo **Tel** (0575) 677736 **Fax** (0575) 677736 **Meals** breakfast, dinner on request **Prices** LL **Rooms** 4 double, 1 single, 3 with bath and shower, central heating, hairdrier, radio, fans **Credit cards** not accepted **Children** not suitable **Closed** Feb **Languages** English, French, some German

Villa apartments, Bagno a Ripoli (Firenze)

Il Palazzo

On the hills of Bagno a Ripoli, 9 km SE of Florence stands this elegant 15thC villa with shady ornamental garden, and beyond that, a discreetly sited swimming-pool with a surprising view of Brunelleschi's cupola. Apartments are stylish and fully equipped. Nearby bus will take you to the centre.

Via Vicinale di Paterno 3, Bagno a Ripoli, 50012 Firenze **Tel** (055) 630127 **Fax** (055) 630127 **Meals** self-catering **Prices** L; one-week minimum stay **Rooms** 5 apartments for 4-8 persons; **Credit cards** not accepted **Children** welcome **Closed** never **Languages** English

Firenze

Farm bed-and-breakfast, Barberino Val d'Elsa (Firenze)

La Spinosa

genuine working farm now run on strict macrobiological
rinciples without the use of herbicides or insecticides. The
one-built farmhouse has been decorated and furnished
ith considerable care and taste (apart from some garish
tted carpets). Horse-riding, swimming-pool and tennis
vailable.

a Le Masse 8, Barberino Val d'Elsa, 50021 Firenze
el (055) 8075413 **Fax** (055) 8066214 **Meals** breakfast, lunch,
nner **Prices** LL-LLL **Rooms** 4 double, 5 suites **Credit cards** V
hildren small children welcome **Closed** Jan to Feb **Languages**
nglish, French, German

Farmhouse apartments, Castelfiorentino

Castello Oliveto

he setting is a magnificent castle of warm red brick that
as played host to popes and royalty and is now mainly used
or functions. Apartments are in nearby restored farmhous-
s surrounded by glorious countryside. Pool, tennis and rid-
g; summer concerts and medieval banquets in the castle.

a di Monte Olivo 6, Castelfiorentino, 50051 Firenze
el (0571) 64322 **Fax** (0571) 61508 **Meals** none **Prices** LL-LLL
ooms 11 apartments for 2-8 persons **Credit cards** EC, MC, V
hildren welcome **Closed** Nov **Languages** English

Country house with apartments, Cortine

Fattoria Casa Sola

ontarsiccio, one of the old farm-houses on the Casa Sola
state (which produces chianti, olive oil and vin santo) has
een pleasantly converted to apartments in classic Tuscan
ustic style, each with its own garden area and access to the
ool beside the main villa. Peaceful rural setting, but also a
seful location for touring. Swimming-pool, horseriding,
ountain bikes.

oc. Cortine, Barberino Val d'Elsa, 50021 Firenze **Tel** (055)
075028 **Fax** (055) 8059194 **Meals** dinner on request
rices L-LL (heating not included); minimum stay of one week
n to Sep **Rooms** 6 apartments sleeping from 2 to 8 persons
redit cards MC, V **Children** welcome **Closed** never **Languages**
nglish, French, Spanish

Firenze

Country villa, Donnini

Villa Pitiana

An enormous and imposing villa in the hills east o
Florence and 12 km from Vallombrosa. It offers 13 doubl
bedrooms and, be warned, 38 apartments. Heavy Empir
style dominates, except in the medieval convent win
Gardens and swimming-pool large enough not to make
seem too crowded. Elegant restaurant.

Loc. Pieve a Pitiana, Donnini, 50060 Firenze **Tel** (055) 860259
Fax (055) 860326 **Meals** breakfast, dinner, snacks **Prices** LLL
(DBB available only, no single room rate) **Rooms**15 double,
all with bath or shower, phone, TV, mini-bar **Credit cards** AE,
DC, EC, MC, V **Children** welcome **Closed** Nov to Mar
Languages English, French, German, Spanish

Country apartments, Fiesole

Fattoria di Maiano

Only 5 km from Florence's centre, but, aside from the vie
(familiar to those who have seen the film *A Room with
View*, which was partially shot there), you could be in dee
countryside. Classily furnished rustic apartments in farm
houses around imposing villa. Small swimming-pool an
shop selling estate's own produce.

Via da Maiano 11, Fiesole, Firenze **Tel** (055) 599600 **Fax** (055)
599640 **Meals** self-catering **Prices** L (heating not included); 3-
night min. stay; one week Mar to Oct **Rooms** 7 fully equipped
apartments for 2-10 persons **Credit cards** EC, MC, V **Children**
welcome **Closed** never **Languages** English, French, German

---

Town hotel, Fiesole

Villa Aurora

Located on Fiesole's famous piazza just across from th
cathedral in a rambling 19thC villa with views from the rea
terrace. Bedrooms vary in size, quality and price; some hav
their own terraces. No. 7 bus to city leaves outside th
entrance. Busy bar next door can be noisy at night.

Piazza Mino 39, Fiesole, 50014 Firenze **Tel** (055) 59100
Fax (055) 59587 **Meals** breakfast, lunch, dinner **Prices** LL-LLL
Rooms 23 double, 2 single, all with bath or shower, phone, TV,
minibar, safe **Credit cards** AE, EC, MC, V **Children** welcome
Closed never **Languages** English

Firenze

Town hotel, Fiesole

Villa Bonelli

notable bargain for accommodation in the centre of
esole (about two minutes' walk to the main piazza and the
us to Florence). The entrance, in a narrow side street, is
ther dark, but the light improves on the upper floors.
uaint old-fashioned furniture clashes with modern pieces.
ood restaurant with view.

a F Poeti1, Fiesole , 50014 Firenze **Tel** (055) 59513, 598941
ax (055) 598942 **Meals** breakfast, dinner **Prices** L-LLL
ooms 23 rooms, all with bath or shower, phone, TV, minibar,
redit cards AE, EC, MC, V **Children** welcome **Closed** restaurant
ly, Nov to mid-Mar **Languages** English, French

Town hotel, Florence

Alba

ot for your honeymoon, but a simple, clean, functional
lace to stay, run by the friendly Caridi family in the his-
oric centre close to the railway station. Rooms are now
ound-proofed against noise from the busy street. Breakfast-
oom is quite stylish except for the curtains on the ceiling.

a della Scala 22/38r, 50123 Firenze **Tel** (055) 282610
ax (055) 288358 **Meals** breakfast **Prices** LL **Rooms** 24, all with
ath or shower, phone, TV, minibar, safe, air-conditioning
redit cards EC, MC, V **Children** welcome **Closed** never
anguages English

City guest-house, Florence

Alessandra

xcellent location in a 16thC palazzo on a quiet street in
e heart of Florence's historic centre is the main attraction
f this modest *pensione*. Some larger rooms, suitable for
milies, are available at very reasonable prices.

rgo SS. Apostoli 17, 50123 Firenze **Tel** (055) 283438
ax (055) 210619 **Meals** breakfast **Prices** LL **Rooms** 6 single (2
ith bath or shower), 19 double (14 with bath); some air-
nditioned **Credit cards** AE, MC, V **Children** welcome **Closed**
o weeks at Christmas **Languages** English, French

Firenze

Town hotel, Florence

Aprile

Originally Palazzo del Borgo, constructed in Medici time
and situated on a street leading away from Piazza S. Mari
Novella, this hotel could have made more stylish use of i
architectural inheritance. Still, there are vaulted ceiling
(some frescoed), a shady courtyard and views of the churc
from some of the bedrooms.

Via della Scala 6, 50123 Firenze **Tel** (055) 216237
Fax (055) 280947 **Meals** breakfast, snacks **Prices** L-LL
Rooms 30, all with bath or shower, central heating, phone,
minibar **Credit cards** AE, EC, MC, V **Children** welcome **Closed**
never **Languages** English

Town hotel, Florence

Ariele

Four bridges down from the Ponte Vecchio, so not tha
central. Oscar Wilde would have had something cruel t
say about the wallpaper in the sitting-room, but elsewher
it is usually simple white plaster enlivened with pottery an
inoffensive paintings. Pleasant gravelled garden with palm
and urns, either for breakfast or for a drink in the evening

Via Magenta 11, 50123 Firenze **Tel** (055) 211509 **Fax** (055)
268521**Meals** breakfast **Prices** L-LL **Rooms** 40, all with bath or
shower, central heating, air-conditioning, TV **Credit cards** AE, E
MC, V **Children** welcome **Closed** never **Languages** English

Town hotel, Florence

Casci

Close to the Duomo and Palazzo Medici-Riccardi in a 15th
palazzo that once belonged to Rossini. However, V
Cavour is one of the city's main bus arteries so, notwit
standing the sound-proofing, ask for a quiet room at th
back. Family run, with a welcoming atmosphere. Breakfa:
room and bar have frescoed ceilings.

Via Cavour 13, 50129 Firenze **Tel** (055) 211686 **Fax** (055)
2396461 **E-mail** CASCI@pn.itnet.it **Website** http://www.emmeti.it/casci.ht
Meals breakfast **Prices** L-LL **Rooms** 25 double, all with bath or
shower, phone, TV **Credit cards** AE, DC, EC, MC, V **Children**
welcome **Closed** never **Languages** English, French, German

Firenze

Town hotel, Florence

City

ı a busy shopping street frequented by Florentine house-
ıves and close to the San Lorenzo tourist market (leather
ɔods and T-shirts) with its many restaurants. The hotel has
ɛen recently renovated, and while the style may not be to
veryone's taste, at least there is a new, clean feel to it, with
lenty of plants and colourful fabrics.

ıa S.Antonino 18, 50123 Firenze **Tel** (055) 211543 **Fax** (055)
95451 **Meals** breakfast **Prices** LL-LLL **Rooms** 18, all with bath
r shower, phone, TV, minibar, air-conditioning **Credit cards** AE,
C, EC, MC, V **Children** welcome **Closed** never
anguages English

Town hotel, Florence

Desiree

lose to the station, which is convenient but not without its
isadvantages, the Desiree is a small *pensione*, carefully man-
ged by its owners, who have decided on a clean, simple
pproach with occasional touches of style. From the pleas-
ıt breakfast-room is a view of Florence's chaotic rooftops.

ia Fiume 20, 50123 Firenze **Tel** (055) 2382382 **Fax** (055)
91439 **Meals** breakfast **Prices** L-LL **Rooms** 26 double, all with
ath or shower, phone, TV; 10 with air-conditoning **Credit**
ards EC, MC, V **Children** welcome **Closed** 2 weeks in Aug
anguages English

Town hotel, Florence

Montebello Splendid

Ɔn grounds of size, we ought not to include this hotel but
ts undeniable, studied elegance will appeal to many of our
eaders who are prepared to pay a little more. The style is
ıeo-classical rather than Florentine, with an emphasis on
ubtle lighting, quiet tones of white, yellow and beige, and
ome fine antiques. Best rooms look on to the garden.

'ia Montebello 60, 50123 Firenze **Tel** (055) 2398051 **Fax** (055)
'11867 **Meals** breakfast, lunch, dinner **Prices** LLL-LLLL
Rooms 39 double, 13 single, 3 suites, all with bath or shower,
ɔhone, TV, minibar, air-conditioning **Credit cards** AE, DC, EC,
ʌC, V **Children** welcome **Closed** never **Languages** English,
rench, German, Spanish

Firenze

Town hotel, Florence

Palazzo Benci

The 16thC palazzo of the historic Benci family has been
converted – somewhat over-zealously, we think – to a
modern hotel. Among its advantages are its prices, which
are reasonable for the city centre and location close to the
church of San Lorenzo. Elegant sitting- and breakfast-
rooms. Bedrooms are standard, with modern comforts.

Via Pz. Madonna Aldobrandini 3, 50123 Firenze **Tel** (055)
217049, 213848 **Fax** (055) 288308 **Meals** breakfast **Prices** LL-
LLL **Rooms** 24 double, 11 single, all with bath or shower, phone
TV, minibar, air-conditioning, **Credit cards** AE, DC, EC, MC, V
Children welcome **Closed** never **Languages** English, French,
German,

Town guest-house, Florence

Pendini

Bull's eye in terms of location: even if you never stay there
you will see Pensione Pendini's sign on the wing of th
'new' (19thC) post office in Piazza Repubblica, where
occupies two storeys. Rooms are spacious and comfortable
avoid those on the piazza, which is full of late-night cafés.

Via Strozzi 2, 50123 Firenze **Tel** (055) 211170 **Fax** (055) 281807
Meals breakfast **Prices** LL-LLL (for triples and family suites)
Rooms 42, all with bath or shower, phone, TV, some air-
conditioned **Credit cards** AE, DC, EC, MC, V **Children** welcome
Closed never **Languages** English, French

Town hotel, Florence

La Residenza

Via Tornabuoni is one of the most fashionable shoppin
streets in Italy, if not in Europe, where the price of a pair c
shoes would cover five nights stay at La Residenza. So d
not expect anything particularly chic, but enjoy the friendl
atmosphere, the flowery roof terrace and the simple, valu
for-money accommodation.

Via Tornabuoni 8, 50123 Firenze **Tel** (055) 284197 **Fax** (055)
284197 **Meals** breakfast, dinner **Prices** L-LL **Rooms** 24, all with
bath or shower, phone, air-conditioning, TV, minibar **Credit card**
AE, DC, EC, MC, V **Children** welcome **Closed** never **Languages**
English

Firenze

Town hotel, Florence

Royal

hotel reasonably close to the centre, with a large garden nsuring peace and quiet and plenty of parking, always has omething to recommend it in this overcrowded city. Mirrors, white marble fireplaces and polished wooden oors add elegance to the public rooms. Bedrooms are more functional, and the singles are decidedly small. Value or money.

Via delle Ruote 52, 50124 Firenze **Tel** (055) 483287, 490648 **Fax** (055) 490976 **Meals** breakfast **Prices** LL **Rooms** 10 single, 0 double, all with bath or shower, phone, TV, minibar, air-onditioning, safe **Credit cards** AE, DC, EC, MC, V **Children** welcome **Closed** never **Languages** English, French, German

Town guest-house, Florence

Silla

Excellent location in the quiet residential area of San Niccolo on the south side of the Arno but within ten min-tes' walk of the main sights. This old-fashioned *pensione* occupies the first floor of a 16thC palazzo and from its spa-ious terrace you can look over the Arno to Florence's amous skyline. Decor will not be to everyone's taste.

Via dei Renai 5, 50125 Firenze **Tel** (055) 2342888 **Fax** (055) 341437 **Meals** breakfast **Prices** LL **Rooms** 32, all with bath or hower, phone, TV, safe, air-conditioning **Credit cards** AE, DC, C, MC, V **Children** welcome **Closed** 2 weeks in Dec **anguages** English

Town hotel, Florence

Splendor

Close to Piazza San Marco and surprisingly swish public ooms for the price, with frescoed ceilings and chandeliers. The breakfast-room, where a copious buffet of fruit, salami, rioches and cereals is served, has elegant painted panels. Bedrooms are more modern but with some respectable pieces. There is a sunny terrace with a view of San Marco.

Via San Gallo 30, 50129 Firenze **Tel** (055) 483427 **Fax** (055) 61276 **Meals** breakfast **Prices** L-LL **Rooms** 31, most with bath r shower; all with phone, TV, safe, hairdrier **Credit cards** EC, MC, V **Children** welcome **Closed** never **Languages** English

Firenze

City guest-house, Florence

Torre Guelfa

New energetic management is making every effort to improve the facilities in this 13thC tower on a quiet street in the city centre. Lovely salon with elaborate wooden ceiling. Bedrooms in blue and green pastel colours, with parquet floors and wrought-iron beds. Bar on top of tower offers knock-out urban views.

Borgo SS. Apostoli 8, 50123 Firenze **Tel** (055) 2396338 **Fax** (055) 2398577 **Meals** breakfast **Prices** LL **Rooms** 5 single (one with bath); 8 double all with bath or shower; 2 rooms air-conditioned; TV on request; minibar **Credit cards** AE, DC, EC, MC, V **Children** welcome **Closed** never **Languages** English, German, French

Suburban hotel, Florence

Villa Belvedere

Hardly an architectural gem, but a pleasant place to retreat to after a day's trekking around the city. Situated on the hill of Poggio Imperiale, beyond the old city gate of Porta Romana, surrounded by trees in well-kept gardens (with pool and tennis) and with views of the town, it has interiors which are modern and comfortable without being exciting.

Via Benedetto Castelli 3, 50124 Firenze **Tel** (055) 222501, 222502 **Fax** (055) 223163 **Meals** breakfast, snacks **Prices** LL-LLL **Rooms** 2 single, 21 double, 3 suites, all with bath or shower, phone, TV, safe, air-conditioning **Credit cards** AE, DC, EC, MC, V **Children** welcome **Closed** Dec to Feb **Languages** English

Town hotel, Florence

Villa Liberty

Turn-of-the-century villa with remnants of the Art Deco style of the period – decorated mirrors, stained glass and ornate lamps. Located some distance from the centre. Ask for a room on the garden side: at weekends, Viale Michelangiolo is busy until the small hours.

Viale Michelangiolo 40, 50125 Firenze **Tel** (055) 6810581 **Fax** (055) 6812595 **Meals** breakfast **Prices** LLL **Rooms** 16 rooms, all with bath or shower, phone, TV, minibar **Credit cards** AE, EC, MC, V **Children** welcome **Closed** never **Languages** English, French

Firenze

Farm guest-house, Galluzzo

La Fattoressa

onvenient if you want to be close enough to Florence for
ay visits, but prefer to spend evenings in country surround-
gs. Rooms, available in the old *casa colonica* (farmhouse)
nd converted outbuildings, are simply furnished, clean
nd comfortable. Bus nearby goes to the centre, avoiding
lorence's nightmare car parking.

ia Volterrana 58, Galluzzo, 50124 Firenze **Tel** (055) 2048418
ax (055) 2048418 **Meals** breakfast, dinner (on request)
rices L-LL **Rooms** 6 double (extra bed possible), all with bath or
hower, heating **Credit cards** not accepted **Children** not small
nes **Closed** never **Languages** English, German, French

Farm guest-house, Greve

La Camporena

lso known as Agriturismo Anna, located 3 km outside
reve on the road to Figline. A tree-lined drive leads up to
his hilltop farmhouse, a position both peaceful and
anoramic with views across the surrounding olive groves.
imple, cheap accommodation, with access to a pleasant
arden and terrace.

ia Figlinese 27, Greve in Chianti, 50022 Firenze **Tel** (055)
53184, 8544765 **Fax** (055) 853184 **Meals** breakfast, dinner
rices L **Rooms** 1 single, 15 double, all with bath or shower
redit cards AE, DC, EC, MC, V **Children** welcome
losed never **Languages** English, German, French

Farm guest-house, Greve

Casa Nova

he town of Greve, capital of Chianti and scene of its annu-
l wine fair, is getting closer to this typical Tuscan farm-
ouse, but you will not notice – most of the views are of hilly
ountryside. Pleasantly proportioned rooms, some with
heir own terraces. Garden to sit in, with the old terracotta
rns once used to store olive oil. A bargain.

ia Uzzano 30, Greve in Chianti, 50022 Firenze **Tel** (055) 853459
Meals breakfast **Prices** L **Rooms** 6 double, all but one with bath or
hower, heating **Credit cards** not accepted **Children** welcome
losed Jan/Feb to Mar **Languages** some English

Firenze

Town hotel, Greve

Chianti

An informal, friendly atmosphere and an enticing swim
ming-pool are the main attractions of this otherwise simpl
hotel located in Greve's principal piazza. The larg
entrance acts as reception, bar, sitting area and breakfas
room. Decent Tuscan food served in the more traditional
styled *trattoria* or on the back terrace.

Piazza G. Matteotti 86, Greve in Chianti, 50022 Firenze
Tel (055) 853763, 853764 **Fax** (055) 853763 **Meals** breakfast,
lunch, dinner **Prices** L-LL (for the suite) **Rooms** 15 double,
1 suite, all with bath or shower, phone, air-conditioning; some
with TV **Credit cards** AE, DC, MC, V **Children** welcome
Closed Nov **Languages** English, French

Country apartments, Montespertoli

Il Molino del Ponte

A somewhat heavy-handed modernization takes awa
from the character of this centuries-old mill belo
Montespertoli. To compensate, everything is spanking ne
in a contemporary Tuscan rustic style. Plenty of sportin
activities available in the area (including an unattractiv
sports complex next door).

Loc. Baccaiano, Via Volterrana Nord 16, Montespertoli, 50025
Firenze**Tel** (0571) 671501 **Fax** (0571) 671435 **Meals** breakfast
Prices L-LL **Rooms** 4 double, 2 single, all with bath or shower,
TV, minibar; 15 studio apartments **Credit cards** EC, MC, V
Children welcome **Closed** never **Languages** English, French,
German

Country guest-house, Pelago

La Doccia

A morning and evening drop off and pick-up service t
Pontassieve railway station for guests wanting a car-free da
in Florence is just one of the advantages of this peacefu
farmhouse. Run by the Mayhew family, it is set in wooc
lands and meadows high in the hills above the Arno valle
and has six traditionally furnished bedrooms, and a pool.

19/20 Ristonchi, 50060 Pelago, Firenze **Tel** (055) 8361387
Fax (055) 8361388 **Meals** breakfast, light lunches, dinner
Prices LL **Rooms** 6 double, all with bath or shower **Credit cards**
MC, V **Children** welcome **Closed** never **Languages** English

Firenze

Country guest-house, Quinto Alto

Podere Novelleto

Situated just beyond Florence's sprawling northern suburb of Sesto Fiorentino, Podere Novelleto is a delightful place to retreat to after a tough day at the city's overcrowded museums. Great view of the city from the pergola on the terrace. Rooms are simply furnished, some in rustic style.

Via Carmignanello 4, Quinto Alto, Sesto Fiorentino, 50019 Firenze **Tel** (055) 454056 **Fax** (055) 451979 **Meals** breakfast, dinner **Prices** L-LL (DB&B) **Rooms** 5 double, all with bath or shower **Credit cards** EC, MC, V **Children** welcome **Closed** never **Languages** English, German, French

---

Country guest-house, Rignana

Fattoria Rignana

At the end of a long unsurfaced road (that starts at the lovely Badia a Passignano) lies this clutter of stone farmhouses and an 18thC villa among unspoilt Chianti countryside. Accommodation is simple but not unstylish (some without own bathroom, however), with the bonus of an excellent *trattoria* (closed Tue) with a fine view over the vineyards.

Loc. Rignana, nr. Badia a Passignano, Greve in Chianti, 50022 Firenze **Tel** (055) 852065 **Fax** (055) 8544874 **Meals** breakfast **Prices** L **Rooms** 7 double, 4 with own bath or shower; 2 apartments for four people **Credit cards** AE, V **Children** welcome **Closed** Nov to Mar **Languages** English, German, French

---

Farm guest-house, Rufina

Fattoria di Petrognano

Magnificently located high in the Rufina hills in the famous Pomino wine-making area, this is very much a place for those who like simple, unstuffy surroundings, a family atmosphere and fine views. Meals are served in the converted stables at a long communal table beneath white arches. Local train to centre of Florence (20 minutes).

Via di Petrognano 40, Pomino, Rufina, 50060 Firenze **Tel** (055) 8318812, 8318867 **Fax** (055) 242918 **Meals** breakfast, lunch (on request), dinner **Prices** L **Rooms** 7 double, most with bath or shower; 5 apartments for 2 to 10 people **Credit cards** not accepted **Children** welcome **Closed** Nov to Easter **Languages** English, French

Firenze

Farmhouse apartments, San Casciano

La Ginestra

True 'Agriturismo': a working farm producing organic pro
duce. Two isolated farmhouses are available, one divided
into apartments (simple rustic style); the other takes groups
of up to 13 people. Peace is assured – it's a long way even to
the nearest bar.

Via Pergolato 3, San Pancrazio, 50020 Firenze **Tel/Fax** (055)
8249245 **Meals** none **Prices** L-LL **Rooms** 5 apartments for 2-6;
one house for 13 (heating not included), all with sitting/dining
room, kitchen, bath, shower, heating, garden, pool **Credit cards**
EU, MC, V **Children** welcome **Closed** never **Languages** English,
German, French, Spanish

Restaurant with rooms, San Casciano Val di Pesa

Antica Posta

A useful touring base situated on the western edge of the
Chianti Classico area, and convenient for Florence, Siena
San Gimignano and Volterra. More famous as a restaurant
than a hotel, the rooms are modern and comfortable but not
particularly stylish. Location on busy road not an advantage.

Piazza Zannoni 1/3, 50026 Firenze **Tel** (055) 822313, 822247
Fax (055) 822278 **Meals** breakfast, lunch, dinner **Prices** L-LL
Rooms 3 single, 7 double all with bath or shower, TV, minibar
Credit cards AE, EC, MC, V **Children** welcome **Closed** never;
restaurant only, Tue (winter) **Languages** English, German,
Spanish

Farmhouse apartments, San Donato in Fronzano

Fattoria degli Usignoli

A spectacular setting 350 m above the Arno Valley makes
this hard to ignore, despite its large size and functionality.
Apartments in the main farmhouse and outbuildings – all
furnished in modern rustic style – are pleasant, but impersonal. Several restaurants, two pools, riding, games room.

San Donato in Fronzano, Donnini, Reggello, 50060 Firenze
Tel (055) 8652018 **Fax** (055) 8652270 **Meals** breakfast,
dinner **Prices** L; DB&B L **Rooms** 40 mini-apartments, with 1 or
2 double bedrooms, shower, kitchenette, sitting/dining room,
heating, phone **Credit cards** AE, EC, MC, V **Children** welcome
Closed Nov to Easter **Languages** English, German

Firenze

Country villa, Strada in Chianti

Villa La Montagnola

A solid 19thC villa which fronts the busy SS222 Chiantigiano road, but benefits from lovely views from its rear. Bedrooms are large, airy and, like the rest of the hotel, well kept. Public rooms are filled with polished wood furniture and a mixed bag of paintings. We found the atmosphere somewhat soulless – no complaints, but no buzz.

Via della Montagnola 110/112, Strada in Chianti, Firenze **Tel** (055) 858485, 8587003 **Fax** (055) 858485 **Meals** Breakfast **Prices** LL **Rooms** 11 doubles, 2 suites; all have bath and shower, TV, minibar, heating, phone **Credit cards** V **Children** welcome **Closed** never **Languages** English, French

---

Country guest-house, Tavarnelle Val di Pesa

Podere Sovigliano

There is a reassuring air about this solid, typically Tuscan farmhouse with its massive walls and old-fashioned dovecot, set in the hilly countryside behind Tavarnelle. Simply furnished bedrooms have independent access to the garden where visitors can relax. Attractive kitchen and sitting-room also open to the family's guests.

Via Magliano 9, Tavernelle Val di Pesa, 50028 Firenze **Tel** (055) 8076217 **Fax** (055) 8050770 **Meals** breakfast, dinner on request **Prices** L-LL (DB&B); 4-day minimum stay **Rooms** 5 double, not all with own bathroom; 1- and 2-bedroom apartments **Credit cards** AE **Children** welcome **Closed** never **Languages** English

---

Farm guest-house, Vico d'Elsa

La Volpaia

Val d'Elsa is becoming almost as popular with tourists as the main Chianti drag with easy access to Florence, Siena, Volterra and San Gimignano. This square 16thC villa and converted farmhouse with pool offers a warm welcome and pleasantly decorated bedrooms. Horses available for country rides. Half-board only.

Strada di Pastine, Vico d'Elsa, 50050 Firenze **Tel** (055) 8073063 **Fax** (055) 8073170 **Meals** breakfast, dinner **Prices** LL (DB&B), *aperitivi* and wine included **Rooms** 10 rooms all with bath or shower **Credit cards** not accepted; travellers' cheques **Children** welcome **Closed** never **Languages** English

Grosseto

Roadside inn, Ansedonia

Locanda di Ansedonia

The address immediately gives away the main defect of thi
otherwise pleasant inn: it is very near the busy Rome
Grosseto highway. Double-glazing has been used to reduc
the nuisance, but try to get a room looking on to the gar
den. A bargain, considering that it is only 15 km from th
chic and costly resorts of Monte Argentario.

Loc. Ansedonia, Via Aurelia Sud (140.5km), Orbetello Scalo,
58016 Grosseto **Tel** (0564) 881317 **Fax** (0564) 881727
Meals breakfast, lunch, dinner **Prices** L-LL **Rooms** 1 single, 11
double, all with bath or shower, air-conditioning **Credit cards** AE,
DC, EC, MC, V **Children** welcome **Closed** Feb **Languages** some
English

Country hotel, Montemerano

Villa Acquaviva

Deep in the heart of the Maremma and close to the therma
springs and mud-baths of Saturnia, this pleasant family-ru
hotel has been furnished with care and taste, using rusti
antiques and bright fabrics. A garden with shady pines an
a terrace, where in fine weather you can eat a deliciou
home-made breakfast, complete the picture. Tennis.

Loc. Acquaviva, Montemerano, 58050 Grosseto **Tel** (0564)
602890 **Fax** (0564) 602895 **Meals** breakfast **Prices** LL **Rooms**
25 double, all with bath or shower; 1 room for the disabled, 7 for
smokers, 2 for pet owners **Credit cards** AE, EC, MC, V **Children**
welcome **Closed** never **Languages** English

Mountain hotel, Montieri

Rifugio Prategiano

A 'rifugio' is normally a mountain hostel with basic facilitie
for tired walkers. This hotel, though still simple, has mor
to offer: a swimming-pool, restaurant, riding excursion
and tennis, as well as an attractive location high in th
Maremma hills. Hearty local food served.

Via Prategiano 45, Montieri, 58026 Grosseto **Tel** (0566) 997703
Fax (0566) 997891 **Meals** Breakfast, lunch, dinner **Prices** L-LL
Rooms 4 single, 20 double, all with shower, phone, TV
Credit cards EC, MC, V **Children** welcome **Closed** Nov to Easter
Languages English

Grosseto

Seaside hotel, Punta Ala

Cala del Porto

Be prepared to pay for the pleasure of being at the centre of Tuscany's chic summer resort. Good facilities (pool, private beach), but you have to pay extra for tennis. Many of the bedrooms have their own terraces with a view of Elba. Staff can be rushed and impersonal in high season.

Via del Porto, Punta Ala, 58040 Grosseto **Tel** (0564) 922455 **Fax** (0564) 920716 **Meals** breakfast, lunch, dinner **Prices** LLLL (DB&B) **Rooms** 41 double, all with bath or shower, phone, TV, minibar **Credit cards** AE, DC, EC, MC, V **Children** welcome **Closed** Oct-May **Languages** English

Seaside hotel, Punta Ala

Piccolo Hotel Alleluja

Punta Ala is the summer home of the Tuscan jet-set, so be prepared to pay over the odds to stay in this yachting-and-boutique town of recent construction, especially in high season. The hotel is 'tasteful-modern' with a private beach. Rooms have either own terrace or private garden.

Via del Porto, Punta Ala, 58040 Grosseto **Tel** (0564) 922050 **Fax** (0564) 920734 **Meals** Breakfast, lunch, dinner **Prices** LLLL (DB&B) **Rooms** 43 double, all with bath or shower, phone, TV, safe, minibar, air-conditioning **Credit cards** AE, DC, EC, MC, V **Children** welcome **Closed** Nov-Mar **Languages** English

Country villa, Saturnia

Villa Clodia

A turn-of-the-century villa on the outskirts of the medieval village of Saturnia, ingeniously constructed around a limestone escarpment that gives great character to the interiors. Some bedrooms have access to a terrace overlooking the valley, and all can enjoy the morning sun pouring in to the light, airy breakfast-room. Thermal springs nearby.

Via Italia 43, Saturnia, 58050 Grosseto **Tel** (0564) 601212 **Fax** (0564) 601212 **Meals** breakfast **Prices** L; 3-day minimum stay; Apr to Oct minimum stay 1 week **Rooms** 2 single, 8 double, all with bath or shower, phone, TV **Credit cards** V **Children** welcome **Closed** 10-20 Dec **Languages** English

Livorno/Lucca

Monhotel

Liberty-style villa dramatically perched above a rocky cove just outside Castiglioncello. Decent, unexciting interiors you will stay here to enjoy the sea air, the private bathing area reached by a lift and the excellent sea-food restaurant Most rooms have a view of the bay.

Via Aurelia 1023, Castiglioncello, 57012 Livorno **Tel** (0586) 752570 **Fax** (0586) 752677 **Meals** breakfast, lunch, dinner **Prices** LL **Rooms** 35 rooms, all with bath or shower, phone, TV **Credit cards** AE, DC, EC, MC, V **Children** welcome **Closed** never **Languages** English, German, French

---

Villa Parisi

Quiet, old-fashioned, family hotel high above a rocky cove surrounded by pine trees. Castiglioncello is a favorite summer place of the Florentine bourgeoisie, and Villa Parisi shares its somewhat staid but relaxed atmosphere. Nice pool in case you find the climb down to the rocks too daunting.

Via della Torre 6, Castiglioncello, 57012 Livorno **Tel** (0586) 751698 **Fax** (0586) 751167 **Meals** breakfast, lunch, dinner **Prices** LL-LLL Rooms 5 single, 15 double, all with bath or shower, phone, TV, minibar, air-conditioning **Credit cards** AE, DC, EC, MC, V **Children** welcome **Closed** never **Languages** English, French

---

Villa La Principessa

The heavy Empire style is understandable when you realize that the villa was once the residence of the Dukes o Bourbon-Parma. Tartan (!) carpets, fabric-covered walls gilt mirrors and draped tables give the interior an over laden air. Pleasant shady gardens and a swimming-pool Traditional food served in the dramatic black dining-room

Loc. Massa Pisana, Via Nuova per Pisa 1616, 55050 Lucc **Tel** (0583) 370037 **Fax** (0583) 379136 **Meals** breakfast, lunch dinner **Prices** LLL-LLLL **Rooms** 5 single, 30 double, 5 suites, a with bath or shower, phone, TV, mini-bar, air-conditionin **Credit cards** AE, DC, EC, MC, V **Children** welcom **Closed** Nov-Mar **Languages** English, German, French

---

Town hotel, Montopoli (Pisa)

Quattro Gigli

Modest but pleasant inn located in the central piazza of Montopoli, where it occupies a 14thC palazzo. More renowned as a restaurant than as a hotel, the bedrooms are fairly standardized; some have views of green valleys. In fine weather, dinner is served on a vine-shaded garden terrace by friendly staff.

Piazza Michele da Monti 2, Montopoli 56020 Pisa **Tel** (0571) 466878 **Fax** (0571) 466879 **Meals** breakfast, lunch, dinner **Prices** L **Rooms** 20 double, all with bath or shower, phone, TV, minibar **Credit cards** AE, DC, EC, MC, V **Children** welcome **Closed** 2 weeks in Nov **Languages** English, French

---

Country villa, Rigoli (Pisa)

Villa di Corliano

Useful location for both Pisa and Lucca, and great value if the battered, aristocratic look is what you like. Public rooms are full of frescoes, chandeliers, statuary. Bedrooms are large but vary in standard; not all have bathrooms. Friendly atmosphere. Famous Pisan chef, Sergio, has a restaurant in the grounds. One visitor was impressed; another found it marred by a lack of comforts.

Via Statale 50, Rigoli, San Giuliano Terme, 56010 Pisa **Tel** (050) 818193 **Fax** (050) 818341 **Meals** breakfast, lunch, dinner **Prices** LL-LLL **Rooms** 18 double, 12 with bath or shower **Credit cards** EC, MC, V **Children** welcome **Closed** never **Languages** English

---

Country hotel, Volterra

Villa Rioddi

Large open spaces spanned by stone arches and brick-vaulted ceilings characterize the ground floor of this 15thC villa just outside Volterra. Furnishing is modern and standardized, with some reproduction rustic. Bedrooms are light, airy and fully equipped. New swimming-pool and garden.

Loc. Rioddi, Volterra, 56048 Pisa **Tel** (0588) 88053 **Fax** (0588) 88074 **Meals** breakfast **Prices** L-LL **Rooms** 9 double, all with bath or shower, phone, TV; 3 apartments for 4 people **Credit cards** AE, DC, EC, MC, V **Children** welcome **Closed** 10 Jan to Mar **Languages** English

Siena

Country hotel, Bagno Vignoni (Siena)

Posta Marcucci

Strongly recommended by a reader, the Posta Marcucci is
new to the guide. It is a simple hotel in a quiet resort village
in the middle of the Orcia Valley, equipped with comfort
able bedrooms, spacious sitting-rooms and a pool filled by
cascades of water from a thermal spring. Tennis, sauna
gym and bowls. Wonderful views, and good value.

Bagno Vignoni 53027, San Quirico d'Orcia, Siena **Tel** (0577)
87712 **Fax** (0577) 887119 **Meals** breakfast, lunch, dinner
Prices L, L-LL (DB&B) **Rooms** 46, all with bath or shower
Credit cards AE, EC, MC, V **Children** welcome **Closed** never
Languages English, Spanish, German

Farm guest-house, Buonconvento (Siena)

Fattoria Pieve a Salti

An appealing choice for those who like the outdoor life
Pieve a Salti is set in 550 hectares of farmland and hunting
reserve which supplies the restaurant with oil, meat, game
and cheese. Six fishing ponds are available for anglers and
a swimming-pool for idlers. Rooms are distributed among
the estate's farmhouses.

Loc. Pieve a Salti, Buonconvento, 53022 Siena **Tel** (0577)
807244 **Fax** (0577) 807244 **Meals** breakfast, lunch, dinner
Prices L, (DB&B) **Rooms** 1 single, 11 double, all with bath or
shower **Credit cards** EC, MC, V **Children** welcome **Closed** never
Languages English, French, German

Country guest-house, Casole d'Elsa (Siena)

Pietralata

Lovely rambling farmhouse in classic Tuscan style 5 km out
side town of Casole d'Elsa, reached by an unsurfaced road
Covered terraces look on to gardens of fragrant rosemar
and woods of holm oak. Bedrooms are simply furnished
with rustic antiques. In the evening the owner presides over
a communal dinner in a lovely brick-ceilinged dining-room

Loc. Pietralata, Via del Teschio 8, Casole d'Elsa, 53031 Siena
Tel (0577) 948657 **Fax** (0577) 948468 **Meals** breakfast, dinner
Prices L **Rooms** 10 double, all with bath or shower **Credit
cards** not accepted **Children** reluctantly accepted **Closed** never
Languages English, German, French

Siena

Farmhouse apartments, Castelnuovo Berardenga

Podere Colle ai Lecci

The Danish owner of this old stone farmhouse makes one of the finest Chianti Classicos, and the house itself is classically Chianti in its location amidst vines, olives and cypresss. Some apartments have their own terraces; others have small private gardens. Wine and oil from the estate on sale.

Loc. San Gusme, Castelnuovo Berardenga, 53010 Siena
Tel (0577) 359084 **Fax** (0577) 358914 **Meals** self-catering
Prices L-LL (heating L25,000 per day); one week minimum stay
Rooms 5 apartments for 2-4 persons; each with kitchen/living room, bedroom and bathroom **Credit cards** DC, V **Children** welcome **Closed** never **Languages** English, Danish

---

Country villa, Colle Val d'Elsa

Villa Belvedere

This time-worn old villa set in its own grounds operates chiefly as a restaurant (especially for weddings and other large functions). Heavy rustic style predominates throughout. Large, well-tended gardens. Food is excellent, and the guest-book is full of appreciative comments. The nearby busy road is a nuisance.

Loc. Belvedere, Colle Val d'Elsa, 53034 Siena Tel (0577) 920966
Fax (0577) 924128 **Meals** breakfast, lunch, dinner **Prices** LL
Rooms 15 double, all with bath or shower, phone, TV
Credit cards AE, DC, EC, MC, V **Children** welcome **Closed** never
Languages English

Village apartments, Fonterutoli

Castello di Fonterutoli

This quaint stone-built village contains some stylishly converted and furnished apartments for weekly rent. Secluded, despite nearby Florence-Siena road (the Chiantigiana). Good restaurant in village that also sells local produce. Swimming-pool.

Loc. Fonterutoli, Castellina in Chianti, 53011 Siena (bookings - Stagioni del Chianti, Via di Campoli 142, Mercatale V d Pesa, FI)
Tel (055) 821481 (bookings) **Fax** (055) 821449 (bookings)
Meals self-catering apartment **Prices** L; one-week minimum stay
Rooms 6 fully-equipped apartments for 4-8 persons **Credit cards** not accepted **Children** welcome **Closed** never **Languages** English

Siena

Farm guest-house, Modanella

Fattoria Godiolo

You will be charmed by the fine upper and lower loggia and tower that form the central part of this old farmhouse devoted to the making of wine, honey and olive oil. Each bedroom has been carefully and individually decorated. Breakfast is with home-made products, and dinner is worth requesting. Useful base for visiting Siena (30 km), Arezzo and Cortona.

Via Modanella Godiolo 22, Rapolano Terme, 53040 Siena
Tel (0577) 704304, no fax **Meals** breakfast, dinner on request
Prices LL **Rooms** 4 double, all with bath or shower
Credit cards not accepted **Children** welcome **Closed** never

---

Town guest-house, Montepulciano

Il Riccio

Located right in the centre of the historic town of Montepulciano, near the Piazza Grande, in an old building going back to the 13thC. Recent restoration has unfortunately removed a great deal of the building's original character. Simple, clean, somewhat Spartan rooms.

Via Talosa 21, Montepulciano, 53045 Siena **Tel** (0578) 757713
Fax (0578) 757713 **Meals** breakfast **Prices** L **Rooms** 5 double, all with bath or shower, phone, TV **Credit cards** AE, MC, V **Children** welcome **Closed** first 10 days in June, first 10 days in Nov **Languages** some French

---

Castle apartments, Monteriggioni

Castel Pietraio

Solid apartments for Tuscan enthusiasts in this imposing, even forbidding, grey medieval stone structure, a few kilometres away from the more elegant defenses of Monteriggioni. Not much to do locally but a good base for reaching Siena, Florence, San Gimignano and Volterra.

Loc. Castel Pietraio, Monteriggioni, 53035 Siena (Via de' Fusari 13, 40123 Bologna – for bookings) **Tel** (0577) 301038; (051) 267534 **Fax** (051) 221376 (bookings) **Meals** self-catering
Prices L; minimum stay: 2 days Oct-May; 1 week Jun-Sep
Rooms 7 full-equipped apartments for 3-5 persons; no pets allowed **Credit cards** not accepted **Children** welcome
Closed never **Languages** little English spoken

Siena

Country hotel, Monticiano

Locanda del Ponte

7thC inn that used to be a stopping-point for the Italian
ost (nobody knows where it stops now). The best rooms
ok on to the River Merse and the ruined bridge that gave
e locanda its name, now the site of the hotel's private
ver beach. Elegant rustic style and appetising food will
ersuade visitors to use it for longer than an overnight stay.

c. Ponte a Macereto, Monticiano, 53015 Siena **Tel** (0577)
7108 **Fax** (0577) 757110 **Meals** breakfast, lunch, dinner
ices L-LLL **Rooms** 23 double, all with bath or shower, phone,
', minibar, air-conditioning **Credit cards** AE, DC, EC, MC, V
ildren welcome **Closed** Feb **Languages** English, German

Farm guest-house, Monti in Chianti

Locanda del Mulino

mple and hospitable converted mill, off the main road
tween Gaiole and Siena (SS 408). Attractive bedrooms in
stic style have access to the grounds which lead down to a
er where the enterprising can go for a swim. Breakfast is
the old mill itself with its machinery still intact.

c. Mulino delle Bagnaie, Monti in Chianti, 53010 Siena
l (0577) 747103 **Meals** breakfast, dinner on request (30,000
 incl. wine) **Prices** L **Rooms** 5 double, all with bath or shower;
ating, telephone **Credit cards** not accepted **Children** welcome
) per cent discount for under-12s) **Closed** Nov to Mar
nguages English, French, German

Country guest-house, Quercegrossa

Mulino di Quercegrossa

converted mill, off the Chiantigiana (the old Florence-
na road) surrounded by paved and terraced gardens. A
ge restaurant and ice-cream parlour make for a lively
nosphere. Prices are reasonable, and the furnishing is a
od example of the modern 'rustic' style. Only 8 km from
na and an hour's drive from Florence.

Chiantigiana, Quercegrossa, 53011 Siena **Tel & fax** (0577)
3129 **Meals** breakfast, dinner **Prices** L **Rooms** 9 double, all
h bath or shower **Credit cards** AE **Children** welcome **Closed**
 to Feb **Languages** English, French

Siena

Country villa, Quercegrossa

Villa Gloria

Rambling hillside villa just off the old road from Florenc
to Siena (Chiantigiana) and only 5 km from the latte
Smart interiors belie the 16thC origins of the farmhous
which has been converted and furnished with a light hanc
Panoramic terrace for breakfast and a swimming-pool fc
relaxation. Value for money.

Loc. Quercegrossa, 53010 Siena **Tel** (0577) 327103
Fax (0577) 327004 **Meals** breakfast **Prices** L **Rooms** 10 double
all with bath or shower; 8 mini-apartments for 2-5 persons
Credit cards AE, DC, EC, MC, V **Children** welcome **Closed** one
week in Dec **Languages** English

Country apartments, Radda in Chianti

Castello di Volpaia

Fortified hilltop village in deepest Chianti, now sadly 'di
covered' by tourists. It produces some prestigious wine
and offers a few compact apartments. Nearby is the Pode
Casetto, more spacious, and with private garden and poc
A quaint bar/grocery in the village sells everyday essentia
local produce and snacks.

Loc. Volpaia, Radda in Chianti, 53017 Siena **Tel** (0577) 738066
Fax (0577) 738619 **Meals** self-catering apartments **Prices** L
Rooms 4 apartments and a farmhouse (with own pool), for 2-8
persons **Credit cards** not accepted **Children** welcome
Closed never **Languages** English

Former coach-house, Rocca D'Orcia

Cantina Il Borgo

Close to the thermal springs of Bagno Vignoni and not I
from Pienza, you will find, in the central piazza of this we
preserved medieval hamlet, the restaurant Cantina
Borgo, which, as well as serving delicious local food, a
has a few stylishly decorated bedrooms for visitors. Used
be the coach-house.

Rocca d'Orcia, 53027 Siena **Tel** (0577) 887280 **Fax** (0577)
887280 **Meals** breakfast, lunch, dinner **Prices** L **Rooms** 3 doub
all with bath or shower, air-conditioning **Credit cards** AE, EC, N
V **Children** welcome **Closed** Feb and one week Nov
Languages English, German

Siena

Country guest-house, San Gimignano

Il Casolare di Libbiano

arefully restored and tastefully furnished old farmhouse
hich combines the advantages of country seclusion with
asy access to San Gimignano and Siena. But if you do not
el like moving, there is a swimming-pool and excellent
cal cuisine on the spot. Bikes for hire.

oc. Libbiano 3, San Gimignano, 53037 Siena **Tel & Fax** (0577)
55102 **Fax** (0577) 955102 **Meals** breakfast, dinner **Prices** LL
ooms 6 double, all with bath or shower, central heating
redit cards AE, MC, V **Children** welcome **Closed** Nov to Mar
anguages English

Converted farmhouse, San Gimignano

La Fornace di Racciano

omfortable converted farmhouse in the countryside just
utside San Gimignano, with a view of the famous towers.
he owners have wisely stuck to the well-tried formula of
rracotta, beams, brick and plaster, with no fancy touches.
lso has an alluring pool, which makes it an excellent bar-
ain for this popular area.

oc. Racciano 6, San Gimignano, 53037 Siena **Tel** (0577)
42156 **Fax** (0577) 942156 **Meals** breakfast **Prices** L-LL
ooms 5 double; all with bath or shower, TV, minibar
redit cards EC, MC, V **Children** welcome **Closed** Nov to Feb
anguages English, French

Farm guest-house, San Gimignano

Il Mattone

n a hill, 5 kilometres north-east of San Gimignano, with
anoramic views. Il Mattone is a wine- and olive-producing
griturismo. Two farm buildings have been turned into a
leasant arrangement of bedrooms and apartments with
eir own little gardens, and all sharing a kitchen, dining
d sitting area. Swimming-pool and tennis court.

oc. Mattone, (strada per Ulignano), San Gimignano, 53037
ena **Tel &fax** (0577) 950075 **Meals** breakfast **Prices** L-LL
ooms 6 double, 4 apartments, all with bath or shower
redit cards not accepted **Children** welcome **Closed** never
anguages English, German

Siena

Country guest-house, San Gimignano

Monchino

A dirt track brings you to this old farmhouse (parts of whic
date back to the 15thC), about 3 km east of San Gimignano
The neat garden, filled with flower pots, has views over th
vines to the town. Simple, light rooms in the converted ha
barn; those in the house have more character. Attractive
situated swimming-pool just below the garden.

Loc. Casale 12, San Gimignano, 53037 Siena **Tel** (0577) 94113€
Fax (0577) 943042 **Meals** breakfast **Prices** L **Rooms** 10 double:
all with bath or shower, minibar **Credit cards** not accepted
Children welcome (only one family room available) **Closed** Dec
to Feb **Languages** English, French

Farm guest-house, San Gimignano

Podere Montese

Dramatically situated on a hillside 1.5 km north of Sa
Gimignano. Visitors will appreciate the warm welcome an
complete peace and quiet of Podere Montese as well as i
swimming-pool complete with panoramic view. Rooms a
modest but pleasant, with white-tiled floors and moder
rustic furniture. The garden terrace makes a pleasant spot

Loc. Fugnano, Via Cellole 11, San Gimignano, 53037 Siena
Tel (0577) 941127 **Fax** (0577) 907350/938856 **Meals** breakfast
Prices L **Rooms** 9 double, all with bath or shower **Credit cards**
not accepted **Children** welcome **Closed** Nov to Mar **Languages**
English, German, French

Country bed-and-breakfast, San Gimignano

Podere Villuzza

A simple farmhouse with a few rooms to offer guests, at th
end of an unsurfaced road 3 km north of San Gimignano
Podere Villuzza is very much a working farm, with vin
growing practically to the door. Nothing fancy about th
accommodation, just pleasant, honest hospitality in a ge
uine rural setting and at reasonable prices.

Loc. Strada 25, San Gimignano, 53037 Siena **Tel** (0577) 94058:
Fax (0577) 942247 **Meals** breakfast, dinner on request **Prices** L
Rooms 4 doubles, all with shower, heating; 3 mini-apartments
with sitting-room and cooking corner **Credit cards** not accepted
Children welcome **Closed** never **Languages** English

Siena

Country hotel, San Gimignano

San Michele

right, up-to-date interiors and the clean lines of the public
eas quickly establish the unfussy style of this hotel.
edrooms are not very large but are well furnished, albeit
ot individually, and each has a new, modern bathroom.
ooms available for the disabled. Enjoyment of the garden
iminished somewhat by the nearby road.

oc. Strada 14, San Gimignano, 53037 Siena **Tel** (0577) 940596
ax (0577) 940596 **Meals** breakfast **Prices** L-LL **Rooms** 14
ouble all with bath or shower, phone, TV **Credit cards** EC, MC, V
hildren welcome **Closed** 8 Jan to 15 Mar **Languages** English,
ench, German

Country hotel, San Gimignano

Sovestro

ist off the busy approach road to San Gimignano (from
oggibonsi) about 2 km out of town. Contemporary hotel
ecoration predominates, though not without hints of style,
ich as the Montechi cotto floor tiling. All rooms have
ither a balcony or a private garden area, plus easy access to
ie swimming-pool.

oc. Sovestro 63, San Gimignano, 53037 Siena **Tel** (0577)
43153 **Fax** (0577) 943089 **Meals** breakfast, lunch, dinner
rices L-LL **Rooms** 1 single, 40 double, all with bath or shower,
hone, TV, air-conditioning **Credit cards** AE, DC, EC, MC, V
hildren welcome **Closed** Feb **Languages** English, French,
erman

Former farmhouse, San Gimignano

Villa Baciolo

easonably priced, simple guest-house only 4 km from San
imignano, with a shady garden and the inevitable view
hich you can enjoy with your breakfast on the terrace.
estoration has been unobtrusive. Bedrooms are surpris-
igly stylish. Impressive brick-vaulted ceilings.

oc. San Donato, San Gimignano, 53037 Siena **Tel & fax** (0577)
42233 **Meals** breakfast **Prices** L; breakfast L9000 **Rooms** 8
ouble, 1 single, all with bath or shower **Credit cards** not
ccepted **Children** welcome **Closed** Nov to Mar
anguages English, German, French

Siena

Villa Belvedere

A 19thC villa redecorated in a light, contemporary styl
which will appeal to those who prefer modern comfort t
time-worn individuality. Gardens are well laid out, wit
palms, olives, cypresses and rosemary bushes, but too clos
to a busy road for true seclusion. The swimming-pool is
bonus at these reasonable prices.

Via Dante 14, San Gimignano, 53037 Siena **Tel** (0577) 940539
Fax (0577) 940327 **Meals** breakfast, dinner **Prices** L **Rooms** 1
single, 11 double all with bath or shower, phone, TV, minibar
Credit cards AE, DC, EC, MC, V **Children** welcome **Closed** never
Languages English

Le Volpaie

Small modern hotel, not without hints of character, in th
suburbs of the nondescript town of Castel San Gimignan
Suitable for an overnight stop if touring in this popula
area. The friendly welcome, comfortable rooms, many wit
their own balconies, garden and reasonable prices mak
this a place not to be overlooked.

Via Nuova 9, Castel San Gimignano, 53030 Siena **Tel** (0577)
953140 **Fax** (0577) 953142 **Meals** breakfast **Prices** L-LL **Rooms**
12 double, 3 single, all with bath or shower, phone, TV
Credit cards AE, DC, EC, MC, V **Children** welcome **Closed** 10
Nov to 10 Mar **Languages** English, some French

Santa Chiara

A 16thC convent stylishly converted into a restaurant an
hotel. The walled garden has an uninterrupted view of th
Valdichiana. Furnishings and decoration show an eclect
mix of styles, with the rustic dominant. The restauran
spanned by brick arches, concentrates on Tuscan cookin
so you will not go hungry.

Piazza Santa Chiara, Sarteano, 53047 Siena **Tel** (0578) 265412
Fax (0578) 266849 **E-mail** rsc@cyber.dada.it **Website**
www.cybermarket.it/rsc **Meals** breakfast, dinner **Prices** L-LL **Rooms** 9
double, 1 suite, all but two with bath or shower **Credit cards** DC
EC, MC, V **Children** welcome **Closed** 10 days in Feb and Nov
Languages English

Siena

Town hotel, Siena

Santa Caterina

Although just on the wrong side of the city walls of Siena, this hotel is always popular. Best bedrooms are on the garden side, with views of the valley and the city while those facing the street have some sound-proofing. Antique furnishing in keeping with the building's character, and marble fireplaces add a welcome note of style.

Via Enea Silvio Piccolomini 7, 53100 Siena **Tel** (0577) 221105 **Fax** (0577) 271087 **Meals** breakfast **Prices** L-LL **Rooms**19 double all with bath or shower, phone, TV, minibar **Credit cards** AE, DC, EC, MC, V **Children** welcome **Closed** 7 Jan to 7 Mar **Languages** English, French

---

Town villa, Siena

Villa Scacciapensieri

On a hilltop 2 km north-east of Siena's historic centre, this 19thC villa has views of both the city's enchanting skyline and the peaceful Tuscan countryside. A formal garden with box hedges keeps at bay recent suburban development. Bedrooms large but unexciting. Shady terrace for outdoor eating, and a swimming-pool for relaxation.

Via di Scacciapensieri 10, 53100 Siena **Tel** (0577) 41441 **Fax** (0577) 270854 **Meals** breakfast, dinner **Prices** LL-LLLL **Rooms** 26 double, 3 single, 2 suites, all with bath or shower, phone, TV, minibar, air-conditioning **Credit cards** AE, DC, EC, MC, V **Children** welcome **Closed** early Jan to mid-Mar **Languages** English, German, French

Perugia

Town hotel, Assisi

Hotel Alexander

This small family-run hotel is tucked away just off the central Piazza del Comune, and offers a useful alternative to
Assisi's pricier central hotels. Its moderate-sized bedrooms
have beamed ceilings and reproduction rustic furniture.
Breakfast is served in the rooms. The Alexander is being
renovated and extended as we go to press, which we understand will add much to the attractions. Reports welcomed.

Piazza Chiesa Nuova 6, Assisi, 06081 Perugia **Tel** (075) 816190
Fax (075) 816804 **Meals** no bar or restaurant facilities **Prices**
rooms L excl breakfast **Rooms** 10 double, 1 suite **Credit cards**
not accepted **Children** accepted **Closed** never **Languages** English

---

Country guest-house, Assisi

Country House

This delightful stone-built guest-house, just below the walls
of Assisi, combines proximity with rural tranquillity.
Signora Silvana Ciammarughi furnishes the comfortable
bedrooms from the stock of the antiques business which
she runs downstairs. Several guests have found her friendly;
some have been put off by her temperamental manner.

San Pietro Campagna 178, Assisi, 06081 Perugia **Tel & fax** (075)
816363 **Meals** breakfast **Prices** L-LL with breakfast **Rooms** 15,
all with bath, central heating. **Credit cards** AE, V, MC **Closed**
never **Languages** English, French, German

Country villa, Assisi Viole

Villa Gabbiano

The country villa of Assisi's ancient Fiumi-Sermattei family
stands in their 150-acre olive estate and has been run as a
guest-house for more than a decade. The present major
rebuilding work, planned for completion in spring 1996,
should make it one of the area's most delightful country
guest-houses. Reports welcome.

Loc. Gabbiano, Assisi, 06081 Perugia **Tel & fax** (075) 8065278
Location S of Assisi – 3 km E of SS147 from Viole; ample
parking **Meals** breakfast, dinner **Prices** DB&B L-LL **Rooms** 9
doubles, 5 singles, 2 apartments in annex **Facilities** sitting-room,
restaurant **Credit cards** none **Closed** never **Languages** French,
some English

Perugia

Town hotel, Castiglione del Lago

Miralago

Despite central position on main piazza, the quiet, spacious rear bedrooms have uninterrupted views over Lake Trasimeno. Most months, the downstairs restaurant, serving fish from the lake as well as meatier, Umbrian dishes, spills on to the lake-view terrace. Proprietors: Patrizi family.

Piazza Mazzini 6, Castiglione del Lago, 06061 Perugia **Tel** (075) 951157 **Fax** (075) 951924 **Meals** restaurant and bar **Prices** rooms L **Rooms** 19 doubles with shower, TV, air-conditioning, minibar, central heating **Credit cards** DC ,V, MC **Children** accepted **Closed** never

---

Town hotel, Città di Castello

Le Mura

Ochre stuccoed walls and shuttered windows, which blend with the surrounding cottages, conceal the hotel's modern construction. Inside, there is no such pretence – comfort and efficiency are regarded as more important. The rear bedrooms have balconies which peep out over the parapet of the city's medieval wall.

Via Borgo Farinario 24, Città di Castello, 06012 Perugia **Tel** (075) 8521070 **Fax** (075) 8521350 **Meals** breakfast, lunch, dinner **Prices** rooms L (breakfast included) **Rooms** 30 double, 5 single, all with bath or shower, TV, minibar, air-conditioning and central heating **Cards** AE, DC, MC, V **Children** accepted **Closed** never **Languages** English, French

---

Converted monastery, Collazzone

Abbazia del Collemedio

A converted monastery in the middle of the countryside between Todi and Perugia which has all the facilities you could wish for, though some might not like the holiday-camp atmosphere. Many attractive original features remain (such as bedrooms made out of monks' cells) but it definitely has the air of a busy hotel. Kidney-shaped swimming-pool.

Loc. Collepepe, Via Convento, Collazzone, 06050 Perugia **Tel** (075) 8789352 **Fax** (075) 8789324 **Meals** breakfast, lunch, dinner **Prices** rooms LL-LLL **Rooms** 57 double, all with bath or shower **Credit cards** AE, DC, EC, MC, V **Children** welcome **Closed** Nov to Mar **Languages** English, French, German

UMBRIA

Perugia

Country guest-house, Gualdo Cattaneo

Il Rotolone

This small guest-house, housed in old farm-workers' co
tages on the Benincasa family estate, commands fine view
out over wooded hills towards Assisi. The moderate-size
bedrooms are simply furnished in appropriate countr
style. The dinner menu makes imaginative use of the farm
organically grown vegetables.

Loc. Sant'Anna, Gualdo Cattaneo, 06035 Perugia **Tel** (0742)
91992 **Fax** (0742) 361307 **Location** between Gualdo Cattaneo
and Bevagna **Meals** breakfast, lunch, dinner **Prices** rooms L wit
breakfast; DB&B L **Rooms** 8, all with shower, TV, heating
Facilities sitting-room, restaurant, bar; garden, riding **Credit
cards** accepted **Closed** never **Languages** some English, French

Town hotel, Gubbio

Bosone Palace

The centre of Gubbio is not exactly brimming over wit
great hotels but the Bosone Palace is a convenient, reason
ably priced place to stay. Attractive entrance and decorate
breakfast-room with vaulted ceiling. Apart from th
Renaissance suite, bedrooms are ordinary but comfortable

Via XX Settembre 22, Gubbio, 06024 Perugia **Tel** (075) 9220688
Fax (075) 9220552 **Meals** breakfast, lunch, dinner **Prices** L-LLL
Rooms 32 double, all with bath or shower, phone, TV, minibar
Credit cards AE, DC, EC, MC, V **Children** welcome
Closed Jan or Feb **Languages** English

Reconstructed castle, Gubbio

Torre dei Calzolari Palace

Great potential on paper, but somewhat disappointing o
inspection. Public rooms are in the original castle that date
back to the 11thC but now with some unfortunate 20th
renovations. Most of the bedrooms, which are standar
modern, in a more recent villa beside. Garden with *putt*
terraces and a pool, quite near a busy road.

Via Torre dei Calzolari, Gubbio, 06020 Perugia **Tel** (075)
9256327 **Fax** (075) 9256320 **Meals** breakfast, lunch, dinner
Prices L-LL **Rooms** 24 double, 4 single, bath or shower, phone,
TV, air-conditioning **Credit cards** AE, DC, EC, MC, V **Children**
welcome **Closed** never **Languages** English, French, German

Perugia

Castle, Scritto di Gubbio

Castello di Petroia

This is about as authentic as you can get: a 13thC castle hardly touched by time (except for the addition of essential modern conveniences) offering a few rooms to travellers. Stark, romantic, isolated on its hilltop, it will appeal to walkers and those in retreat from modern life. Heavy rustic furniture predominates.

Loc. Petroia, Scritto di Gubbio, 06024 Perugia **Tel** (075) 920109, 920287 **Fax** (075) 920108 **Meals** breakfast, dinner on request **Prices** L-LL Rooms 4 double, 1 suite, all with bath or shower **Credit cards** not accepted **Children** welcome **Closed** Jan to Mar **Languages** English

Island hotel, Isola Maggiore

Hotel Da Sauro

A short boat trip from Tuoro or Passignano takes you to Isola Maggiore and a renowned restaurant that also offers the island's only hotel accommodation. The bedrooms are small, pine-furnished and somewhat characterless, but the Scarpocchi family's hospitality, the fish menu and the lake views more than compensate.

Via Guglielmi 1, Isola Maggiore, 06060 Perugia **Tel** (075) 826168 **Fax** (075) 825130 **Meals** breakfast, lunch, dinner **Prices** Rooms L **Rooms** 10 doubles with shower, 2 apartments; all centrally heated **Credit cards** DC, V **Children** accepted **Closed** 3 weeks in Nov and mid-Jan to mid-Feb **Languages** French, Spanish

Farm guest-house, Nocera Umbra

La Valle

Off the main Perugia-Assisi drag but still accessible, visitors will enjoy the peaceful hilltop location of this 18thC stone farmhouse, the dining-room with its long wooden tables and wine-barrels and the reasonable prices. Accommodation is simple but adequate and the surrounding countryside makes for some lovely drives.

Loc. Colle, Nocera Umbra, 06020 Perugia **Tel** (0742) 810329 **Fax** (0742) 810666 **Meals** breakfast, lunch, dinner **Prices** L **Rooms** 4 double, two bathrooms shared **Credit cards** AE **Children** welcome **Closed** never **Languages** some English

Perugia

Village hotel, Paciano

Locanda della Rocca

In the remarkably preserved medieval village of Paciano
Luigi Buitoni and his wife, Caterina, have turned an ol
olive press into an attractive restaurant (cooking course
available), and given over seven bedrooms in their palazz
to guests. Their style and taste makes the most of the buil
ings' characteristic features without stinting on comfort.

Viale Roma 4, Paciano, 06060 Perugia **Tel** (075) 830236
Fax (075) 830155 **Meals** breakfast, lunch, dinner **Prices** LL
Rooms 7 double, all with bath or shower **Credit cards** AE, DC,
EC, MC, V **Children** welcome **Closed** Jan to Feb; restaurant,
never **Languages** English

Town hotel, Perugia

Brufani

Imposing foyer with plush couches and copies of classica
statues set in wall niches. Unusually for a town hotel, som
of the bedrooms have views of the Umbrian countryside
stretching to Assisi and Todi on the horizon. Refine
atmosphere and high prices attract an up-market clientèle.

Piazza Italia 12, 06100 Perugia **Tel** (075) 5732541 **Fax** (075)
5720210 **Meals** breakfast, lunch, dinner **Prices** LLL-LLLL
Rooms 3 single, 16 double, 5 suites, all with bath or shower,
phone, TV, minibar, air-conditioning, safe **Credit cards** AE, DC,
EC, V **Children** welcome **Closed** never **Languages** English

---

Town hotel, Perugia

Locanda della Posta

Prime location on Perugia's renowned Corso Vanucc
where the Perugini religiously take their evening *passegiata*
Famous as a hotel for more than two hundred years, its pre
vious guests included Goethe, Hans-Christian Anderser
and Frederick III of Prussia. Rooms are stylish.

Corso Vanucci 97, 06100 Perugia Tel (075) 5728925
Fax (075) 5722413 **Meals** breakfast **Prices** LL-LLLL
Rooms 12 single, 26 double, 1 suite, all with bath or shower,
phone, TV, minibar, central heating, air-conditioning
Credit cards AE, DC, EC, MC, V **Children** welcome **Closed** never
Languages English, French

Perugia

Farm guest-house, Pietralunga

La Cerqua

An excellent bargain for those who like the quiet rural life. Situated in panoramic northern Umbria between Citta di Castello and Gubbio and decorated in authentic rustic style, guests of La Cerqua can enjoy long walks in the oak forests between meals of hearty Umbrian fare. Small lake or fishing nearby.

Loc. San Salvatore, Pietralunga, 06026 Perugia **Tel** (075) 9460283 **Fax** (075) 9462033 **Meals** breakfast, lunch, dinner **Prices** L **Rooms** 5 double, 2 suites, all with bath or shower **Credit cards** AE, EC, MC, V **Children** welcome **Closed** Jan **Languages** English, French

Country hotel, Spoleto

Il Barbarossa

Very reasonably priced for such swanky furnishing (black leather, antiques, marble) but this may be a new hotel's bid for customers. We preferred the interiors, which are finely done, to the exterior, which is bare and excessively lit for the extensive car park. This is no more than a useful back-up address: reports welcome.

Via Licina 12, Spoleto, 06049 Perugia **Tel** (0743) 43644 **Fax** (0743) 222060 **Meals** breakfast, lunch, dinner **Prices** L-LL **Rooms** 1 single, 9 double, all with bath or shower, phone, TV, minibar, air-conditioning **Credit cards** AE, DC, EC, MC, V **Children** welcome **Closed** never **Languages** English, French

Former convent, Todi

Bramante

A useful address just outside Todi, below Bramante's famous church. The 14thC convent has been modernised with none too light a hand, but some character remains. The restaurant is more stylish than the other public rooms and has a fine terrace with a view. Most bedrooms are standard, with a few exceptions. Swimming-pool; tennis court.

Via Orvietana 48, Todi, 06059 Perugia Tel (075) 8948381/2 **Fax** (075) 8948074 **Meals** Breakfast, lunch, dinner **Prices** LL-LL **Rooms** 40 double, 1 single, two suites, all with bath or shower, phone, TV, air-conditioning, minibar **Credit cards** AE, DC, EC, MC, V **Children** welcome **Closed** never **Languages** English

Town hotel, Todi

Fonte Cesia

Could have been a great hotel – a 17thC palace right in the heart of Todi – but we felt that modernization had been taken too far, overwhelming the original character of the building with excessive plushness and jarring contemporary decoration. But do not be too put off: it's value for money and right outside is Todi.

Via Lorenzo Lonj 3, Todi, 06059 Perugia **Tel** (075) 8943737 **Fax** (075) 8944677 **Meals** breakfast, lunch, dinner **Prices** LL **Rooms** 32 double, 2 singles, 5 suites, all with bath or shower, phone, TV, minibar, air-conditioning **Credit cards** AE, DC, EC, MC, V **Children** welcome **Closed** never; restaurant only, Wed **Languages** English, French, German

Self-catering castle apartments, Valfabbrica

Castello di Giomici

The 12thC hamlet which makes up Castello di Giomici tops a wooded hill above the peaceful valley of Valfabbrica. Much of it has now been converted by Luciano Vagni into self-catering apartments, each furnished with smart rustic simplicity. Garden, swimming-pool. No nearby restaurants.

Il Castello di Giomici, 06029 Valfabbrica, 06029 Perugia **Tel** (075) 901243 **Fax** (075) 901713 **Meals** none **Prices** apartments L, minimum3 nights **Rooms** 4 apartments, for up to 8 **Facilities** each apartment has bedroom, bathroom, sitting-room cooking facilities **Credit cards** none **Children** accepted **Closed** never **Languages** English, German, Dutch

Restored hamlet, Ficulle (Terni)

La Casella

La Casella, a hamlet of 12 houses built from local stone in the wooded hills north of Orvieto and isolated from the rest of the world by 7 km of unsurfaced road, is definitely for those in search of peace and quiet. A convivial atmosphere. Communal dining, attractive bar plus swimming-pool, tennis.

Loc. Ficulle, 05016 Terni **Tel** (0763) 86075 **Fax** (0763) 86684 **Meals** breakfast, lunch, dinner **Prices** L-LL (DB&B) LLL (full board) **Rooms** 15 double, all with bath or shower **Credit cards** AE, DC, EC, MC, V **Children** welcome **Closed** never **Languages** English, French, Spanish, Danish

Terni

Country hotel, Montefranco

Fonte Gaia

Useful overnight accommodation for those travelling towards the Central Appennines. Pretty enough on the outside, although the fading Sixties interior is in need of refit. A change of management is anticipated – reports welcome.

loc. Racognano, 05030 Montefranco, 05030 Terni **Tel** (0744) 388621 **Fax** (0744) 388598 **Meals** breakfast, lunch, dinner **Prices** rooms L with breakfast **Rooms** 16 double, 2 single, suites, all with bath or shower, television, minibar, central-heating **Credit cards** AE, DC, MC, V **Closed** never **Languages** English, French, German

---

Town hotel, Narni

Il Minareto

Surely Umbria's quirkiest hotel: once a 14thC monastery, it was converted into a Moorish villa at the end of the 19thC. Even the old campanile resembles a minaret. Very comfortable modern bedrooms and an excellent restaurant.

Via dei Cappuccini Nuovi 32, Narni, 05035 Terni **Tel** (0744) 726343 **Fax** (0744) 726284 **Meals** breakfast, lunch, dinner **Prices** rooms L **Rooms** 5 double, 3 singles, all with bath or shower, air-conditioning, TV, minibar, central heating **Credit cards** AE, DC, MC, V **Closed** never; restaurant only, Wed **Languages** some English, French

Reporting to the guide

Reporting to the guides
Please write and tell us about your experiences of small hotels, bed-and-breakfasts and inns, whether good or bad, whether listed in this edition or not. As well as hotels in Tuscany and Umbria, we are interested in charming small hotels in: Britain, Ireland, Italy, France, Spain, Portugal, Germany, Austria, Switzerland and other European countries, as well as the east and west coasts of the United States.

The address to write to is:
The Editor
Charming Small Hotel Guides
Duncan Petersen Publishing Ltd
31 Ceylon Road
London W14 0PY
England

Checklist
Please use a separate sheet of paper for each report; include your name, address and telephone number on each report.
   Your reports will be received with particular pleasure if they are typed, and if they are organized under the following headings:
   Name of establishment
   Town or village it is in, or nearest
   Full address, including post code
   Telephone number
   Time and duration of visit
   The building and setting
   The public rooms
   The bedrooms and bathrooms
   Physical comfort (chairs, beds, heat, light, hot water)
   Standards of maintenance and housekeeping
   Atmosphere, welcome and service
   Food
   Value for money

We assume that in writing you have no objection to your views being published unpaid, either verbatim or in an edited version. Names of major outside contributors are acknowledged in the guide, at the editors' discretion.

Index of hotel names

Index of hotel names

Index of hotel names

Index of hotel names

Index of hotel locations

Index of hotel locations

Index of hotel locations

Index of hotel locations

Special Offer

uy your **Charming Small Hotel Guide** by post directly from
e publisher and you'll get a worthwhile discount. *

itles available:	Retail price	Discount price
ustria	£9.99	**£8.50**
ritain & Ireland	£9.99	**£8.50**
ritain: **Most Distinctive Bed & Breakfasts**	£9.99	**£8.50**
SA: Florida	£9.99	**£8.50**
ance	£9.99	**£8.50**
ance: *Bed & Breakfast*	£8.99	**£7.50**
ermany	£9.99	**£8.50**
aly	£9.99	**£8.50**
SA: New England	£9.99	**£8.50**
aris	£9.99	**£8.50**
outhern France	£9.99	**£8.50**
pain	£8.99	**£8.50**
vitzerland	£9.99	**£8.50**
uscany & Umbria	£9.99	**£8.50**
enice	£9.99	**£8.50**

so available: Duncan Petersen's **Independent Traveller's
uides:** outstanding all-purpose travel guides.

itles available:	Retail price	Discount price
ustralia	£12.99	**£10.50**
alifornia	£12.99	**£10.50**
entral Italy	£12.99	**£10.50**
orida	£12.99	**£10.50**
ance	£12.99	**£10.50**
reece	£12.99	**£10.50**
aly	£12.99	**£10.50**
pain	£12.99	**£10.50**
hailand	£12.99	**£10.50**
urkey	£12.99	**£10.50**
ngland & Wales		
Walks Planner & Guide	£12.99	**£10.50**

ease send your order to:

Book Sales, Duncan Petersen Publishing Ltd,
31 Ceylon Road, London W14 OPY
   enclosing: 1) the title you require and number of copies
   2) your name and address 3) your cheque made out to:
Duncan Petersen Publishing Ltd
   *Offer applies to UK only.

Hotel Special Offers

CHARMING SMALL HOTEL GUIDES

Would you like to receive information about special discounts at hotels in the
Charming Small Hotel Guide
series?

Many of our hotels are offering big savings on standard room rates if you book at certain times of the year.

If so, send your name and address to:

Reader Information
Charming Small
Hotel Guides
Duncan Petersen Publishing
31 Ceylon Road
London W14 0PY

For more offers see page 191